MW01711493

Nelson International Mathematics

Pupil's Book 4

OXFORD
UNIVERSITY PRESS

OXFORD
UNIVERSITY PRESS

Great Clarendon Street, Oxford, OX2 6DP, United Kingdom

Oxford University Press is a department of the University of Oxford. It furthers the University's objective of excellence in research, scholarship, and education by publishing worldwide. Oxford is a registered trade mark of Oxford University Press in the UK and in certain other countries

First published by Nelson Thornes Ltd in 2010

British Library Cataloguing in Publication Data
Data available

978-1-4085-0776-6

10 9 8

Printed in Great Britain by Bell & Bain Ltd, Glasgow

Acknowledgements

Cover: Andy Peters
Illustrations: Alan Rogers and Pantek Arts Ltd, Maidstone, Kent
Page make-up: Pantek Arts Ltd, Maidstone, Kent

Photo acknowledgements
iStockphoto: pp34, 50, 54, 68, 78, 79, 114

Although we have made every effort to trace and contact all copyright holders before publication this has not been possible in all cases. If notified, the publisher will rectify any errors or omissions at the earliest opportunity.

Contents

Contents

How quickly can you add?

Answer these questions about the picture. Try to work them out in your head. Then write the number sentences in your exercise book.

1 How many children are skipping?

2 How many children are playing games with a ball?

3 If the tennis players joined in skipping, how many would be skipping?

4 How many children are there altogether?

5 Find four groups that can be put together to make 30.

6 Find five groups that can be put together to make 20.

7 List all the groups which could be put together to make 11.

8 How many groups of six could all the children make? Would any be left over?

you can use Workbook page 4

Word scores

Boubacar gave each letter of the alphabet a score from 1 to 9.

A	B	C	D	E	F	G	H	I	J	K	L	M	N	O	P	Q	R	S	T	U	V	W	X	Y	Z
1	2	3	4	5	6	7	8	9	1	2	3	4	5	6	7	8	9	1	2	3	4	5	6	7	8

Each word gets a score, like this:

M A T H S

4 1 2 8 1 $\quad 4 + 1 + 2 + 8 + 1 = 16$

The word score for 'maths' is 16.

1 Make three more words with a score of 16.

2 What is the score for your name?

3 What is the score for your friend's name?

4 Do longer names always have a bigger score?

5 Which has the highest score, 'huge' or 'tiny'?

6 Do a class survey of name scores.

7 Yasmin turned over these cards.

1	2		4	5			8	

She used these rules:

- Use each card only once for each sum.
- Only add numbers.

a Can she make every number between 10 and 20?

b How many different ways can she make 16?

c Investigate different ways of making other numbers.

Compare and order using < and >

< means 'less than', e.g. 100 < 105

> means 'greater than', e.g. 105 > 100

1 Copy and complete. Fill in < or >.

a 99 [ ] 150 **b** 21 [ ] 7

c 439 [ ] 98 **d** 760 [ ] 19

e 499 [ ] 501 **f** 85 [ ] 300

2 Use these number cards.
Write:

a three number sentences using <

b three number sentences using >.

45 100 638 249 75 728

3 Write each set of numbers in order from smallest to greatest.

a 720, 659, 985, 460, 302

b 118, 102, 108, 111, 150

c 907, 970, 709, 790, 799, 797

you can use Workbook page 5

Sticks and intersections

You can solve multiplication problems by laying out sticks.

This one shows 4 × 6

There are four sticks with six sticks laid over them. Everywhere the sticks cross there are intersections.

There are 24 intersections: 4 × 6 = 24

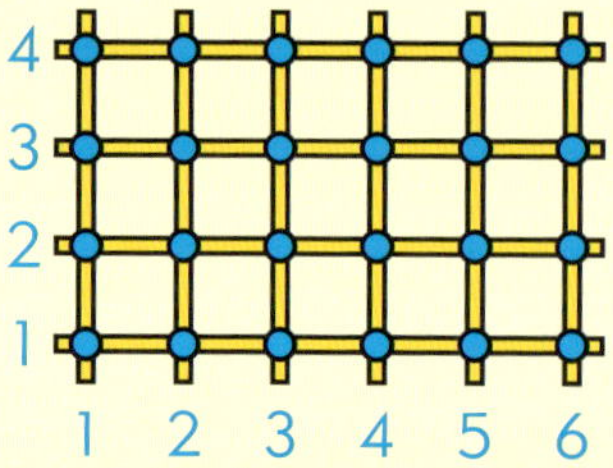

1 **Use sticky tape and some straws or sticks. Tape together sticks to make the intersections to show each of these:**

a 5 × 7 35	**b** 8 × 8 64	**c** 3 × 9 27
d 6 × 8 48	**e** 4 × 10 40	**f** 8 × 9 72
g 7 × 7 49	**h** 9 × 5 45	**i** 10 × 6 60

2 **You might notice that the sticks not only make intersections, they also make squares of open space.**

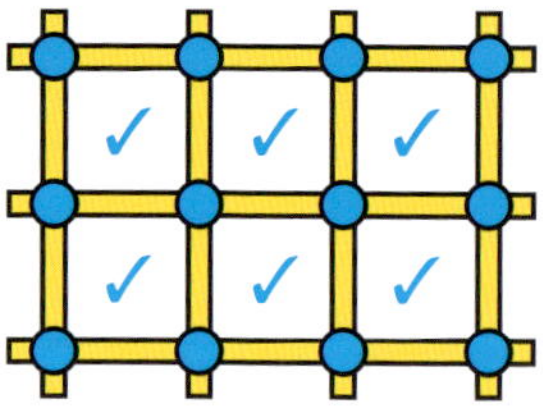

The ticks [✓] show the squares of open space.

Use sticks or straws to investigate other arrangements, such as 2 × 4 or 5 × 4.

2 x 4 = 8
5 x 4 = 20

Make a chart showing the arrangement of the number of intersections and the number of squares. Do you notice any patterns? dot, stick, dot, stick

How many ways?

The arrangement of dots below is called a **multiplication array**. Look at these facts about the number 24.

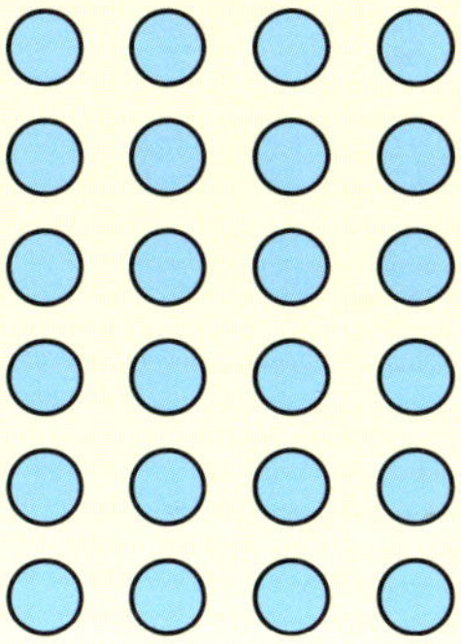

6 rows of 4 = 24

4 rows of 6 = 24

$6 \times 4 = 24$ $4 \times 6 = 24$

$4 + 4 + 4 + 4 + 4 + 4 = 24$

$6 + 6 + 6 + 6 = 24$

$24 \div 4 = 6$ $24 \div 6 = 4$

1 **Write all the facts about these arrays.**

a

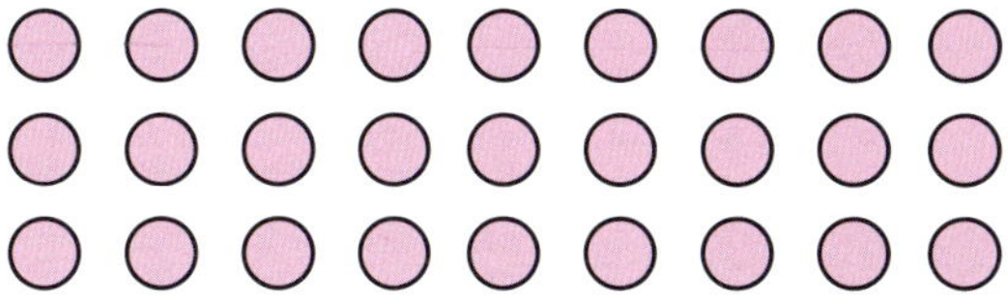

3x8=24 3rows of 8
8x3=24 8 rows of 3

b

5x8=40 8x5=40 5rows of8 8rows of5

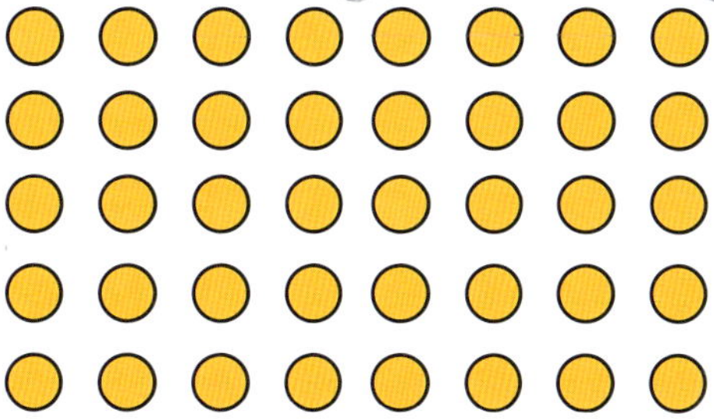

c

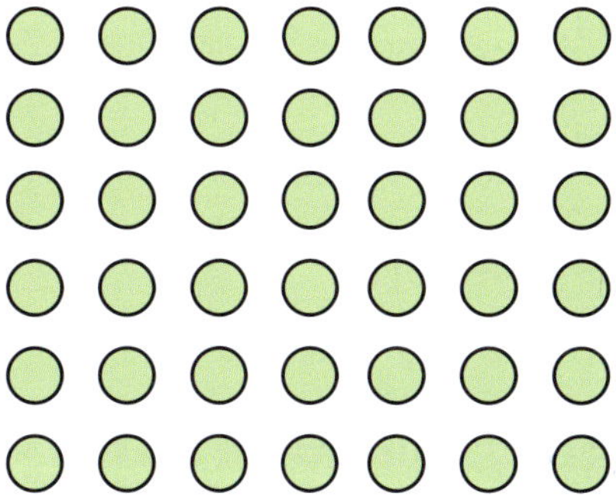

6 rows of 7 7 rows of 6 6x7=76

d

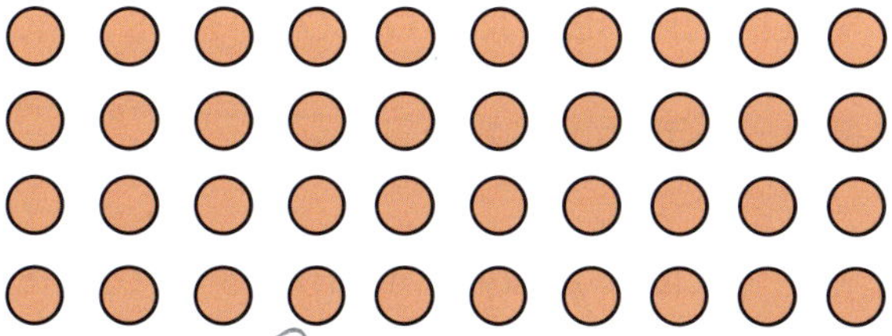

4x10=40
10x4=40

2 **Use buttons, beads or stones to show these numbers as arrays.**

a 32 **b** 45 **c** 48 **d** 36

you can use Workbook pages 6–7

Code breakers

×	6	9	7	4
5	O	W	T	V
8	E	L	M	A
3	U	S	D	I
10	N	C	P	K

This grid shows a code.
To use it, you multiply two numbers to find a letter.

$5 \times 4 = 20$

20 is the code for V

1 Use the grid above to break this code.

45 48   72 3×4 40 8×6

56 18 9×8 35 12 70 72 4×3 90 32 5×7 12 30 60

8×4 6×10 3×7   21 12 20 12 3×9 3×4 5×6 60

Use the grid to make your own coded message.

Ask a friend to decode it.

You will need: 10 counters and a stopwatch.

2 Table strips game

Each player makes a table strip like the one on page 6 of the Workbook, with all the numbers filled in.

Decide on how many numbers on the strip will be covered. The first player places counters on the strip. The other player has ten seconds to work out which numbers are covered. This player removes the counters from those numbers which are correct.

The score is the number of counters collected. Swap over. Now the other player must try to collect counters. The player with the most counters is the winner.

you can use Workbook pages 8–9

Investigating polygons

A **geo-board** is a piece of board with nails or pegs arranged on it in a grid. You can use it to make polygons. A **polygon** is a shape with straight sides.

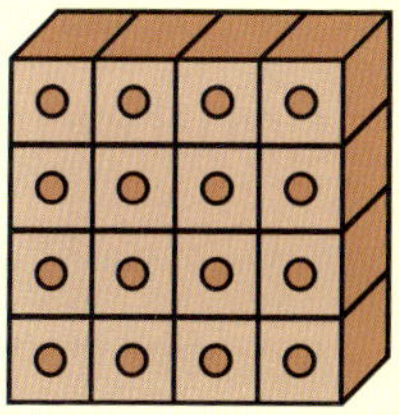

1 Use geo-boards or spotty paper to make these polygons. Write their names.

a
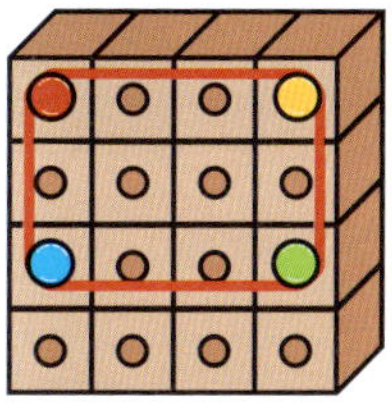

b
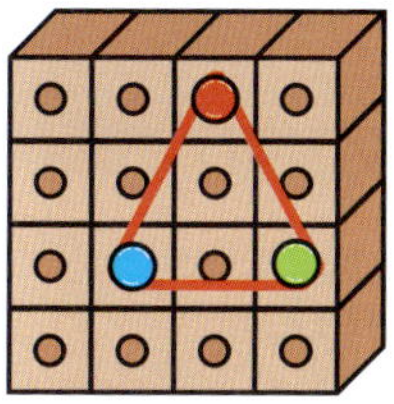

c

d
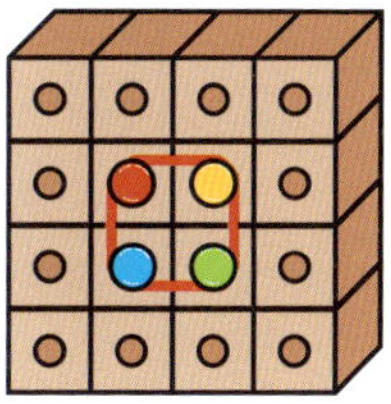

e

f
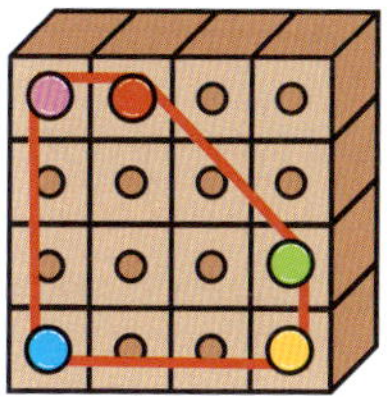

2 Find out what these road signs mean. Write what shape they are.

a

b

c

d

3 Which shapes are the most common for traffic signs in your area?

you can use Workbook pages 10–11

Investigating rectangles

You will need:

- geo-boards of different sizes
- elastic bands
- spotty paper
- used matchsticks or craftsticks.

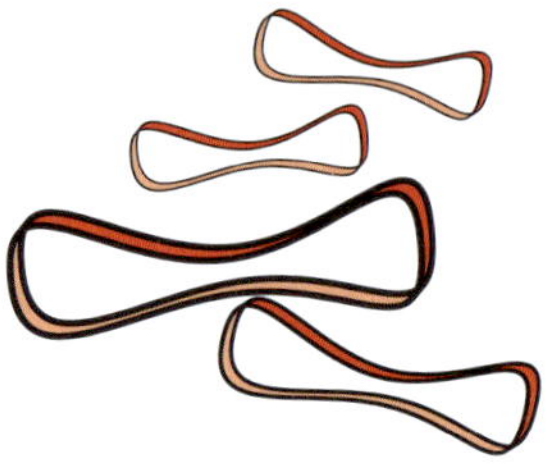

1 Use a 9-pin geo-board.

a How many different-sized squares can you make?

b How many other rectangles can you make?

2 Now use a 16-pin geo-board.

a How many different sized squares can you make?

b How many other rectangles can you make?

c Experiment with other geo-boards.

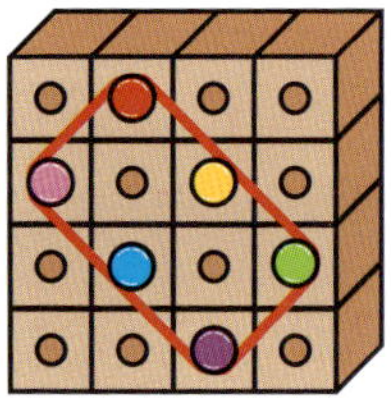

**3 Make these patterns and solve the puzzles.
Draw the new pattern.**

a

Remove 2 matches to leave just 2 squares.

b

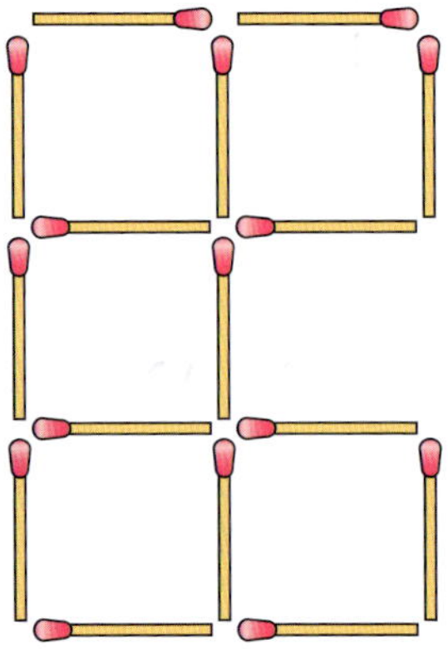

Move 3 matches to make 4 squares.

c

Move 2 matches to make 6 squares.

you can use Workbook page 12

Solids and their nets

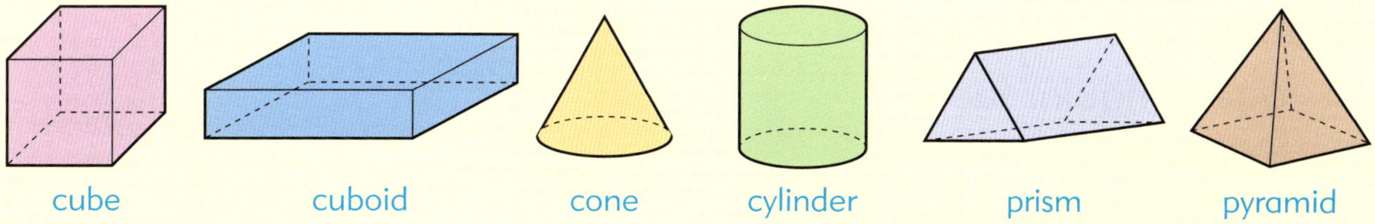

A **net** is a flat shape that you can fold to enclose a solid shape.

1 Say what solid each net would enclose when you fold it up. Copy the shapes and make your own net for each shape.

a

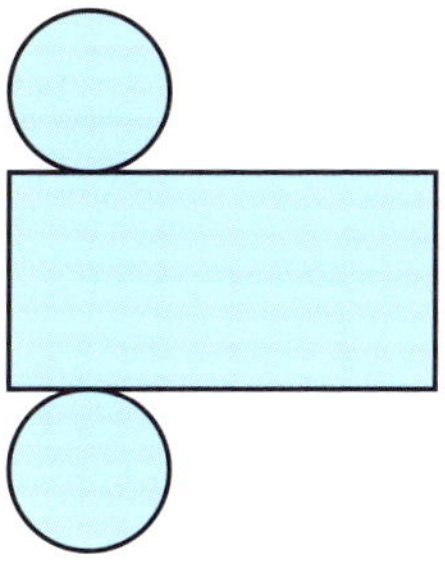

b

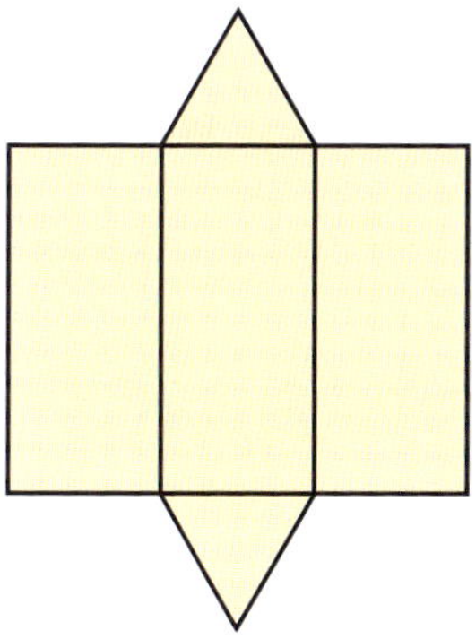

c

d

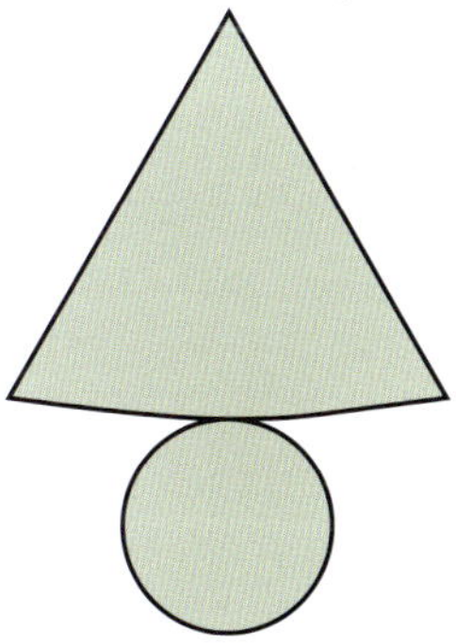

e

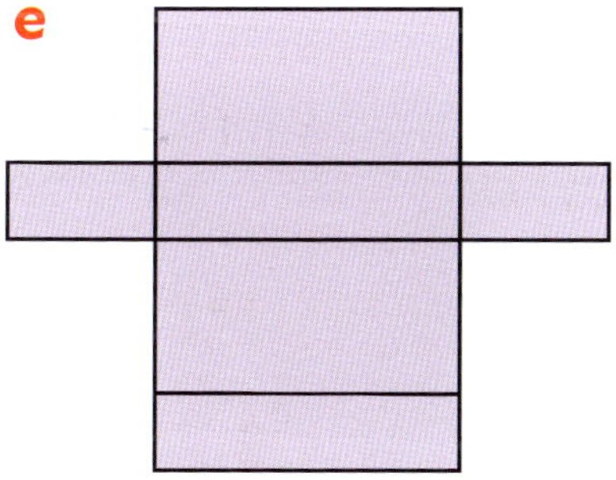

f

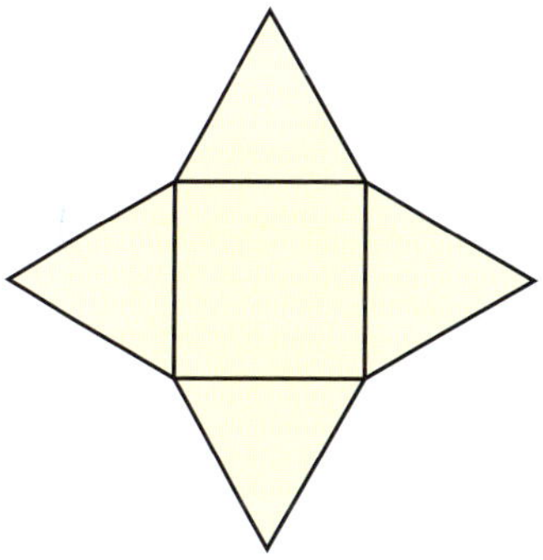

2 Use squared paper. Choose one of the solids above and draw two different ways of making its net.

Is it a cuboid?

A cuboid has:

- 6 rectangular faces
- right-angled vertices
- opposite faces that are the same size and shape.

A **cube** is a special sort of cuboid because all its faces are identical.

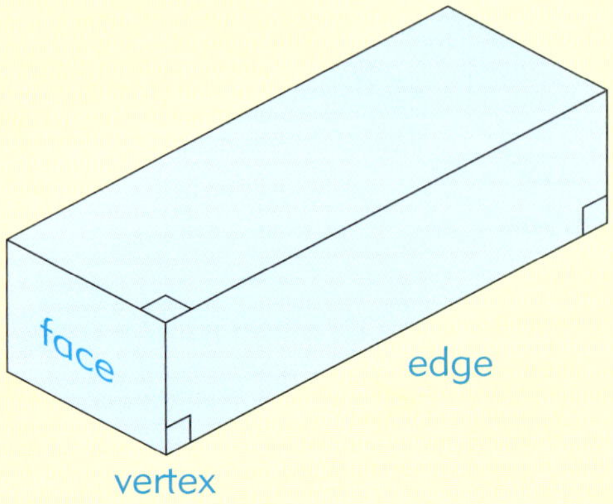

1 Say which of these shapes will make a cube or cuboid.

a

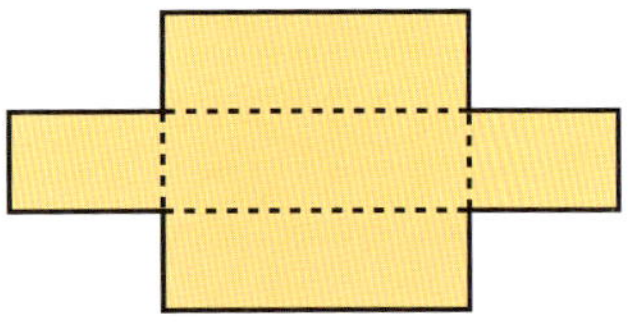

b

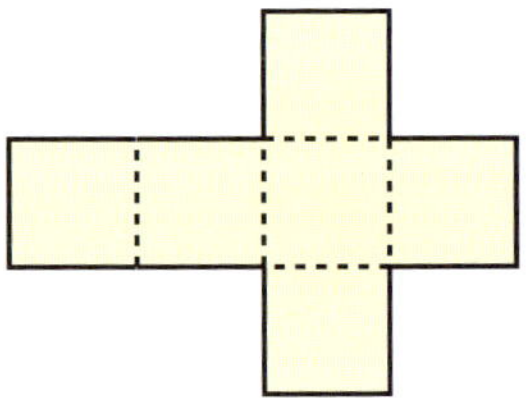

c

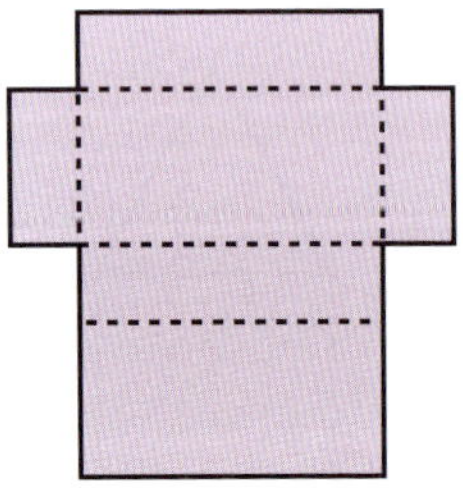

d

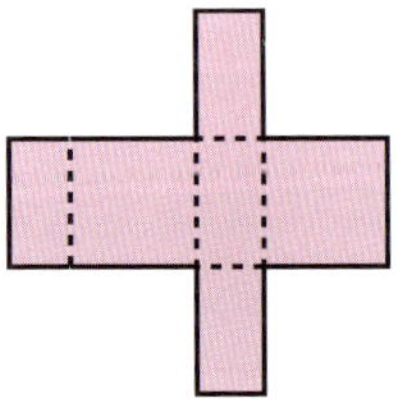

e

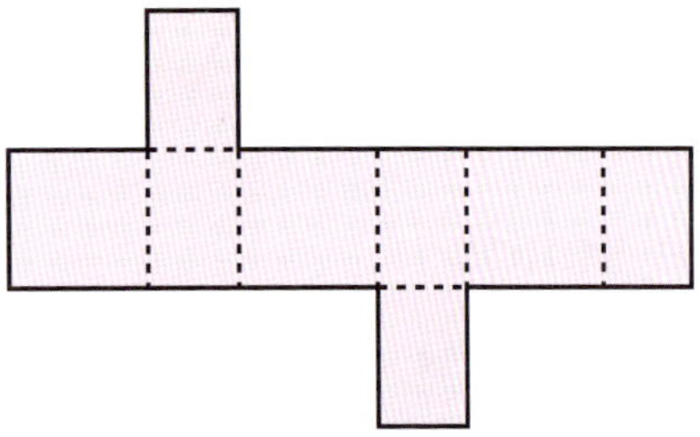

g

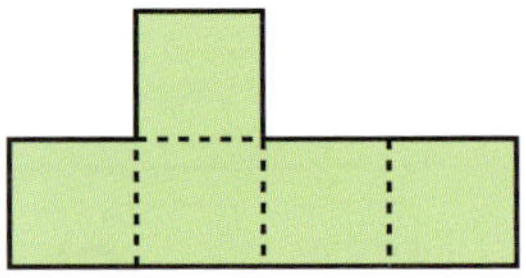

2 Draw each net, cut it out and try to make the shapes.

Is it a pyramid?

The base of a pyramid is a polygon. All the other faces are triangles that meet at a point. We name each pyramid according to the shape of its base.

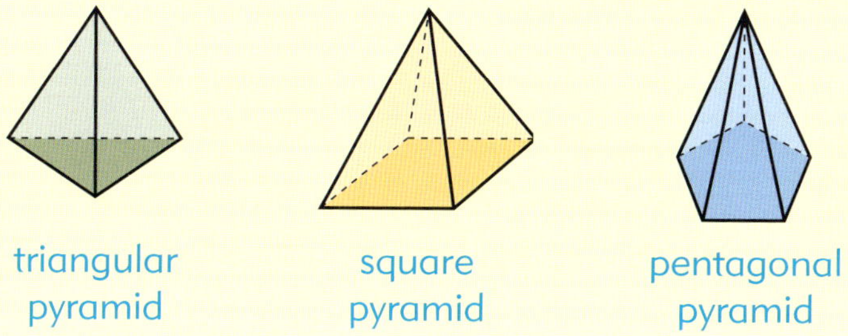

1 Say which of these shapes are nets of pyramids.

a
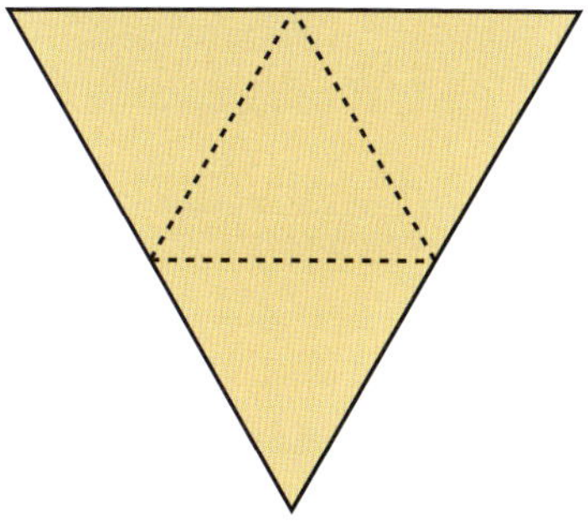

b
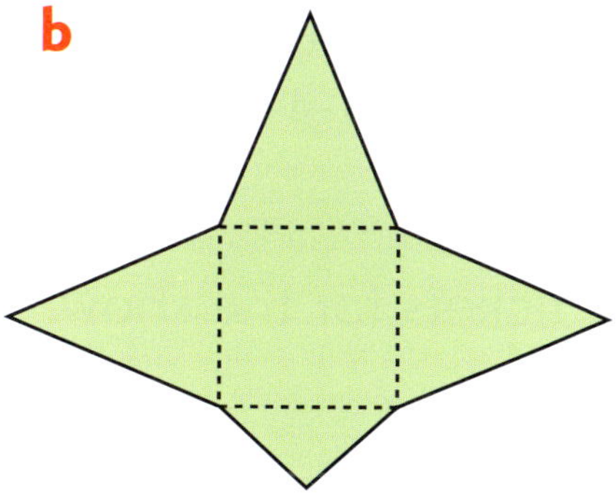

c
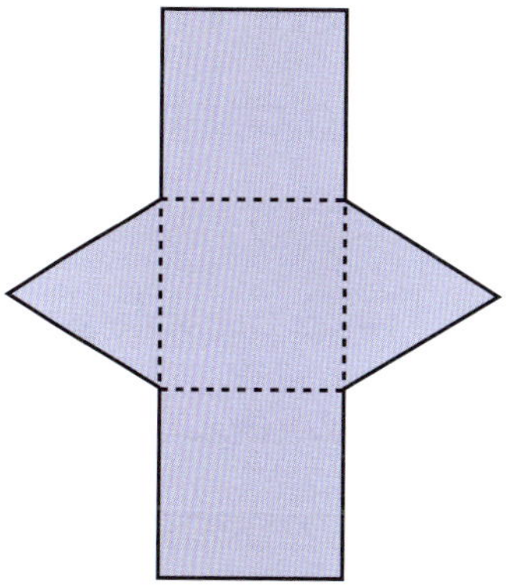

d
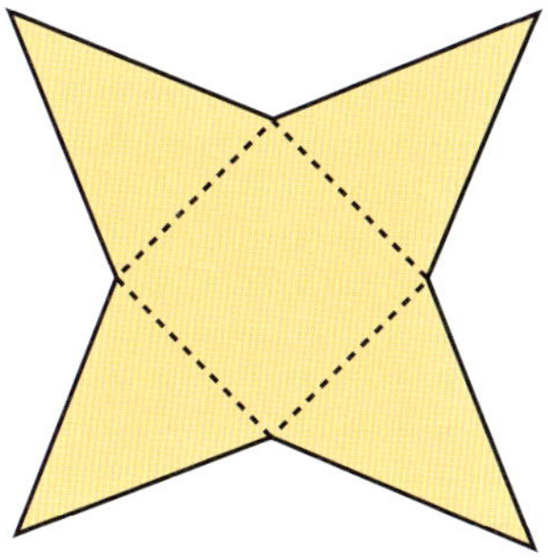

e
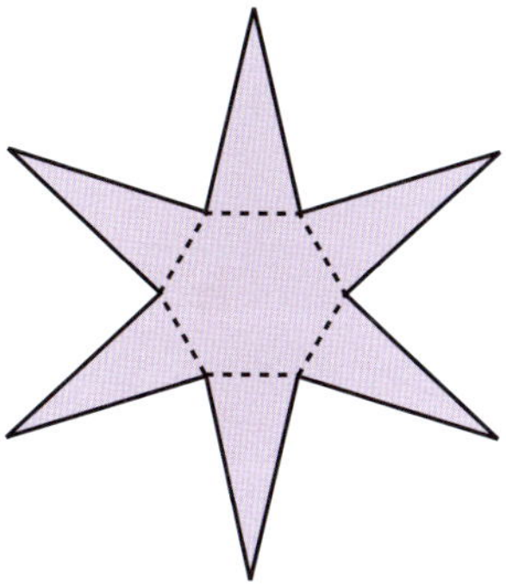

f
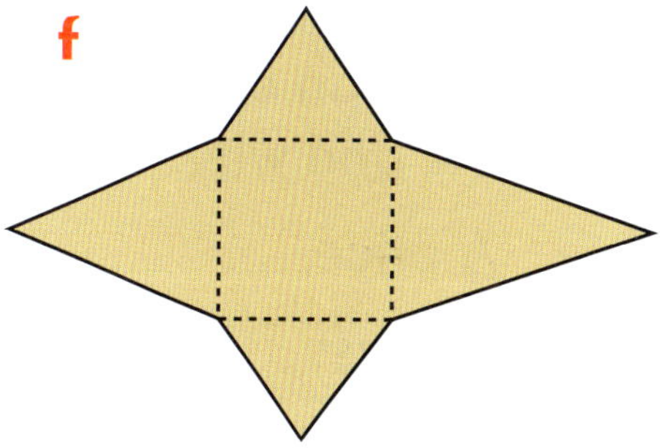

2 Draw each net, cut it out and try to make the shapes.

Rounding off to the nearest ten

Is it nearer to the next ten or the ten before?

If the units are 4 or fewer, round down.

If the units are 5 or more, round up.

27 is <u>about 30</u>.

24 is <u>about 20</u>.

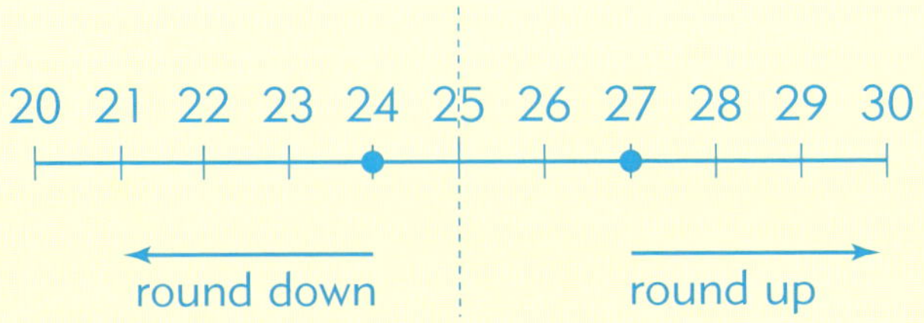

1 **Round each number to the nearest ten. You can draw number lines to help you.**

a There were 48 people at the party.

b The car took 52 litres of petrol.

c Jamal made 85 cupcakes.

d 142 people bought tickets for the show.

e I have 276 books.

f 405 people wrote letters of complaint.

2 **Give an example of when you might round it off and why.**

a A price.

b A height measurement.

c A mass.

d A time.

3 **Should each person round up or down? Give a reason for each answer.**

a A seamstress needs 8.4 metres of fabric for some curtains. The fabric is sold in full metres.

b A caterer needs 6 kg of flour to make the bread for a party. Flour is sold in 5 kg bags.

you can use Workbook page 13

Remainders

Divide the fish into groups of 6.

$32 \div 6 = 5$ remainder 2

We can write this as 5 r. 2

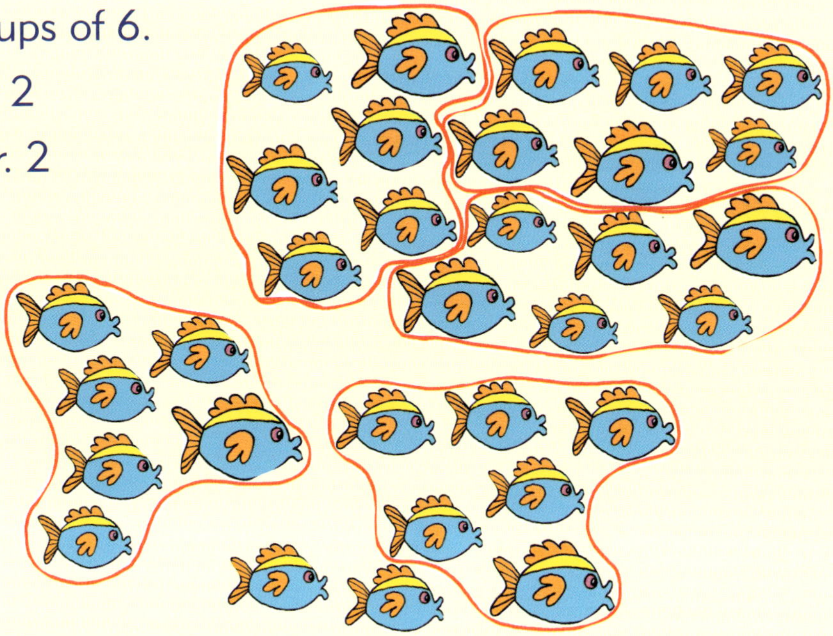

1 **Can you split the group of fish into groups of 5? Write out the division sum, with the remainder.**

2 **Try to split the 32 fish into groups of:**

a 2 **b** 3 **c** 4

d 7 **e** 9 **f** 10

Write each division sum with a remainder if necessary.

3 **Try this with the number of pupils in your class.**

a Split the total class into groups of 2, 3, 4, 5, 6, 7, 8, 9, 10.

b Write each division sum with a remainder if necessary.

you can use Workbook page 14

Rounding off after division

There are 52 beans in the jar. I divide them among 5 people. How many beans does each person get?

52 ÷ 5 = 10 remainder 2

Each person gets about 10 beads.

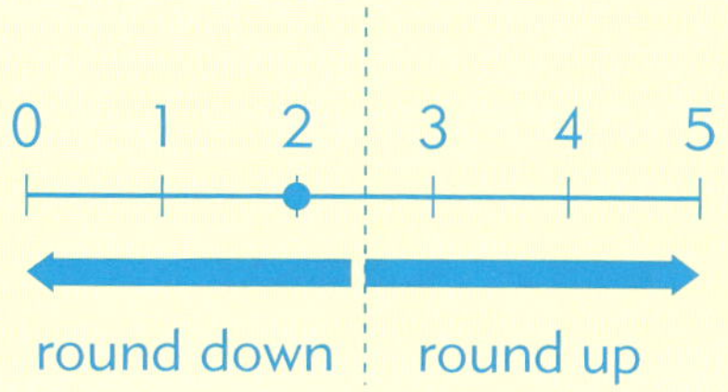

Divide. Round off.

1

among 3 groups

2

among 7 groups

3

among 9 groups

4

among 10 groups

5

among 5 groups

6

among 8 groups

Multiply by 100

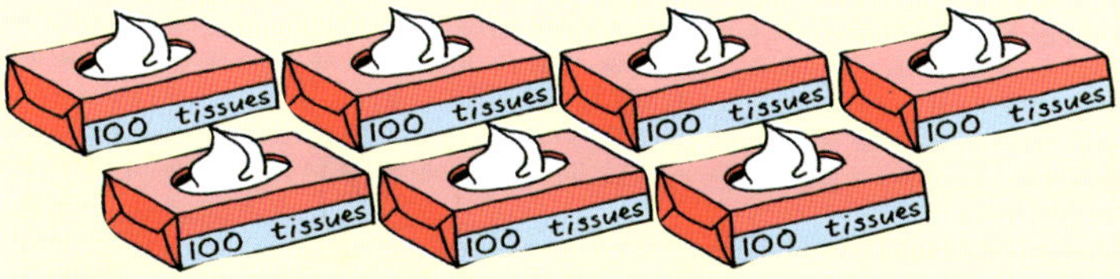

$7 \times 100 = 700$

$12 \times 100 = 1200$

When you multiply a number by 100, your answer has two zeros at the end. In other words, the place value of the number you are multiplying moves up by two places.

1 **Write the first ten multiples of 100.**

2 **A pair of jeans costs $100. How much are the following?**

a 2 pairs of jeans

b 3 pairs of jeans

c 5 pairs of jeans

d 7 pairs of jeans

e 9 pairs of jeans

f 11 pairs of jeans

3 **Look at these three sums:**

$5 \times 1 = 5$ $5 \times 10 = 50$ $5 \times 100 = 500$

a Discuss with a partner the patterns you notice. How can this help you when you multiply by 1, 10 or 100?

b What happens when you divide by 1, 10 or 100? What rules or patterns can you use to help you?

4 **Name three things that we might use or buy in packs of 100.**

Measuring angles

To use a protractor to measure angles, place the centre of the protractor on the vertex of the angle. Line up the base line of the protractor with one arm of the angle. Start at 0 on the base line. Read the number of degrees on the other arm.

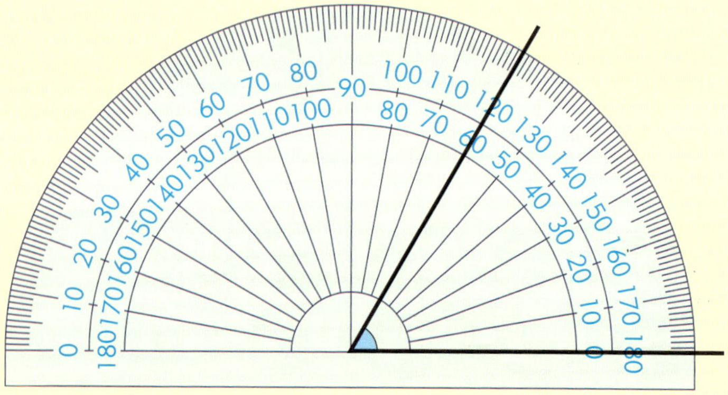

This angle measures 60°.

Use a protractor to measure all of the angles in each of these shapes. Add up the angles in each shape. You may need to trace the shapes and extend the sides to measure the angles. What do you notice?

1

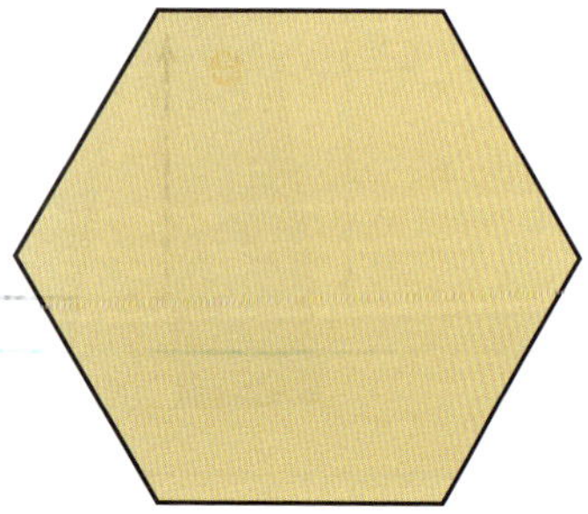

2

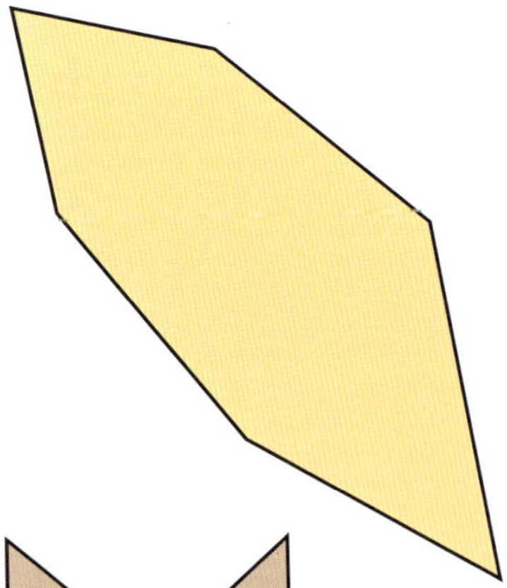

3

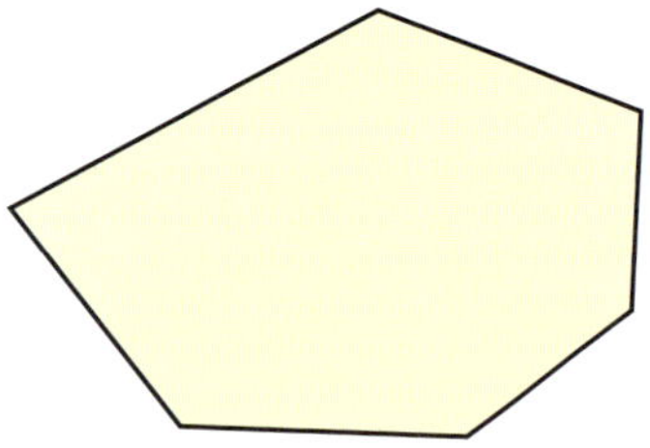

4

you can use Workbook pages 15–16

Measuring angles in degrees

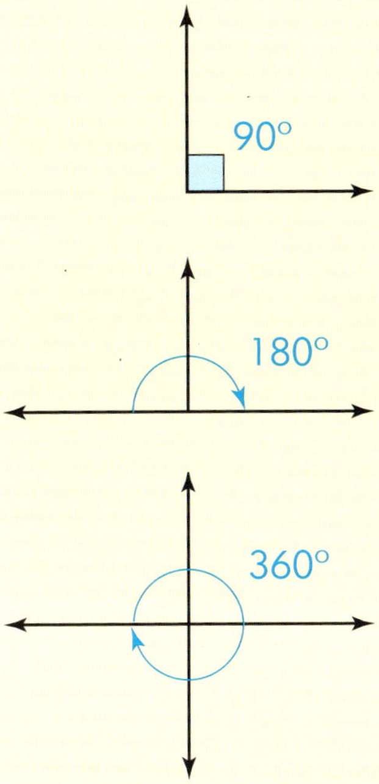

45° half a right angle

90° a right angle or square corner

180° two right angles make a straight line

360° four right angles make a full turn

A protractor is an instrument for measuring angles.

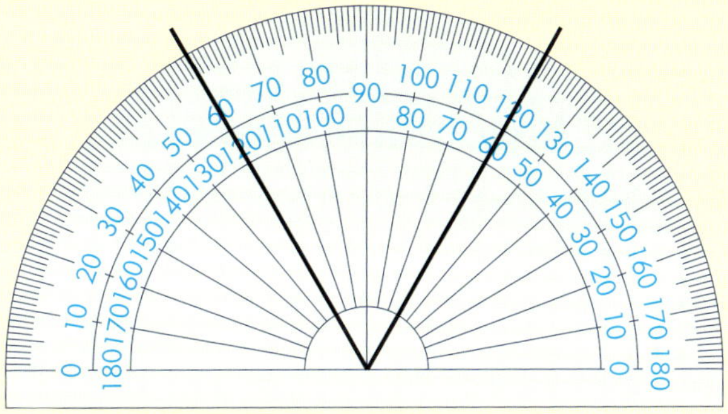

1 Write the letters of the right angles in your exercise book.

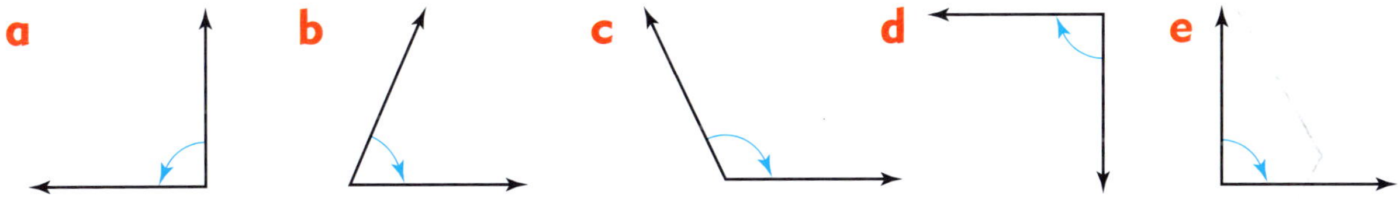

2 Do you think each of these angles is greater than, equal to or less than 90°?

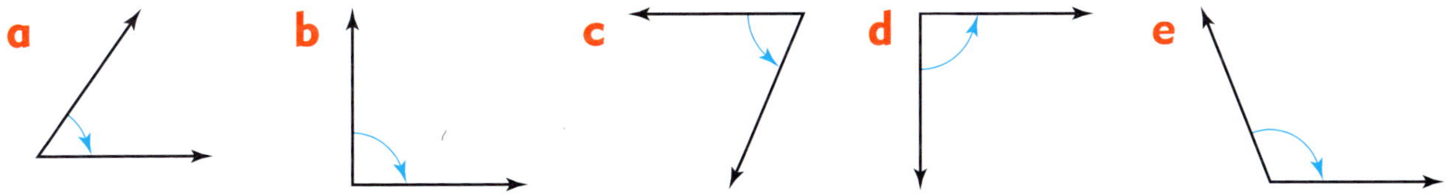

3 Use a protractor to measure each angle.

4 Find three angles in your classroom that are:

a equal to 90° **b** greater than 90° **c** less than 90°

you can use Workbook page 17

Checking out angles

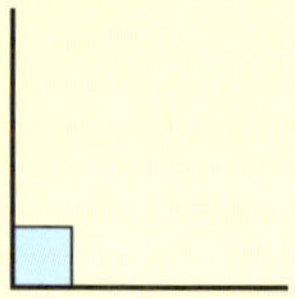

right angle
90°

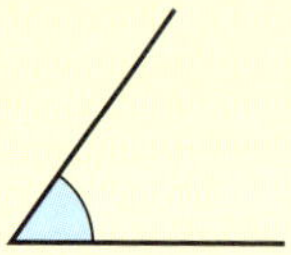

acute angle
less than 90°

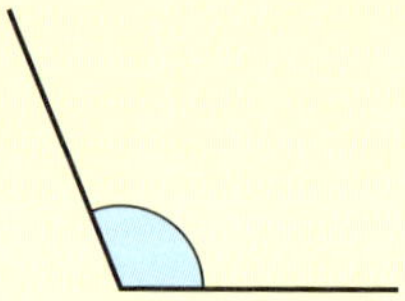

obtuse angle
greater than 90°

1 **Write down how many acute, obtuse and right angles each shape contains.**

a

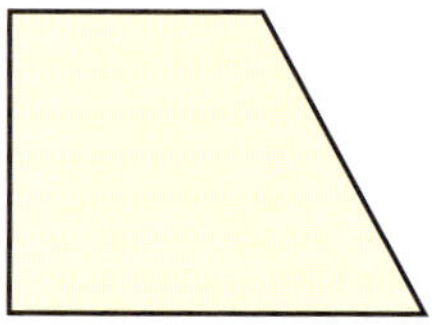

b

c

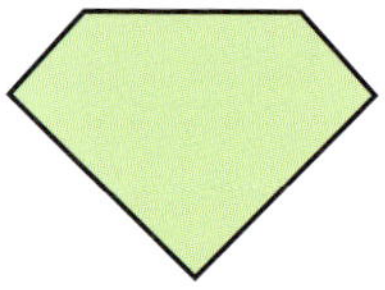

d

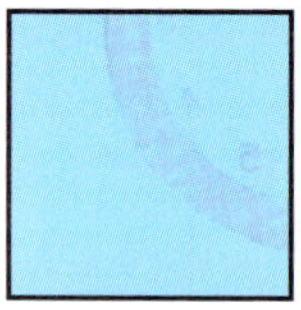

e

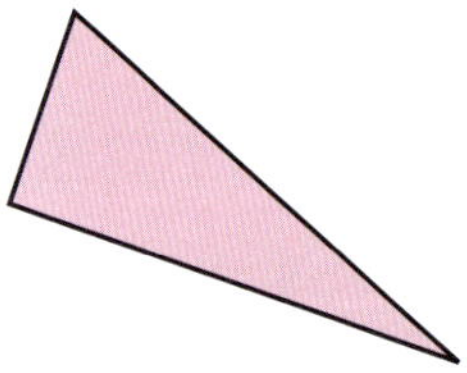

f

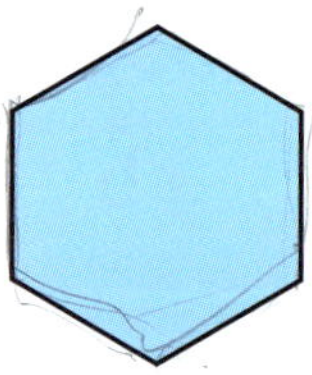

2 **Are these angles 90°, less than 90° or more than 90°?**

Estimate how many degrees each angle has.

a

b

c

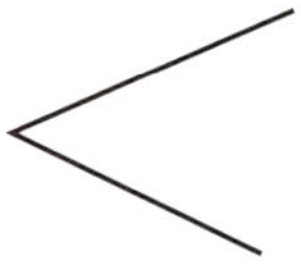

d

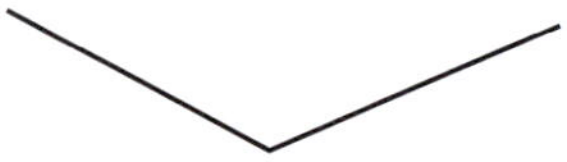

e

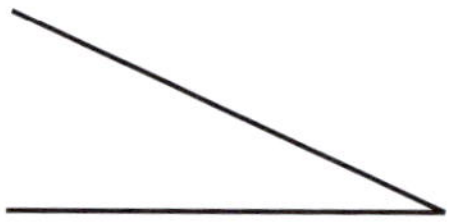

f

you can use Workbook pages 18–19

Time angles

The hands on a clock face make different angles, according to the times they show.

1 **Say whether each angle is a right angle, acute angle or obtuse angle.**

a

b

c

d

e

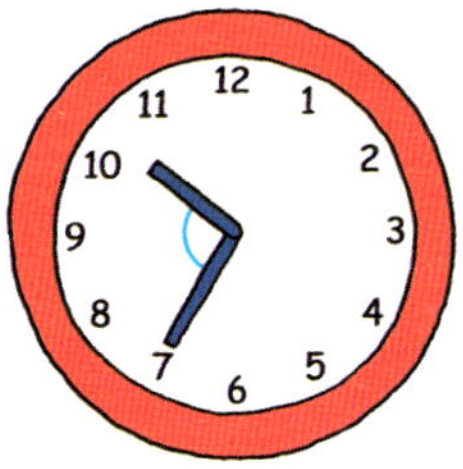

f

2 **Draw clock faces to show these times.**

What sort of angles do the hands make?

a 5:05 **b** 3:30 **c** 11:50

d 6:15 **e** 6:05 **f** 2:40

3 **Look for angles in your classroom.**

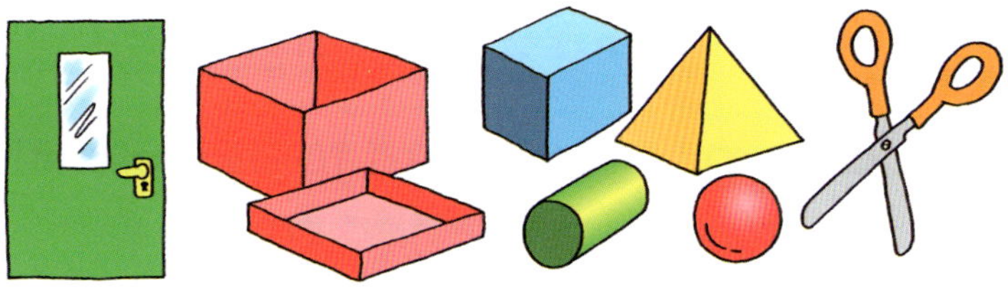

a Find three right angles, three acute angles and three obtuse angles.

b Write the names of the items, or draw them.

Geo-board investigations

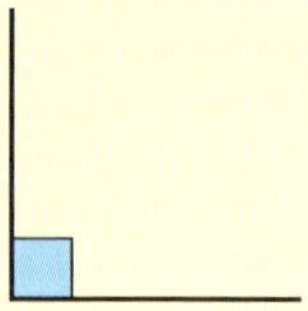

Remember: A right angle measures 90°.

The shape on this geo-board has 4 right angles and 4 sides.

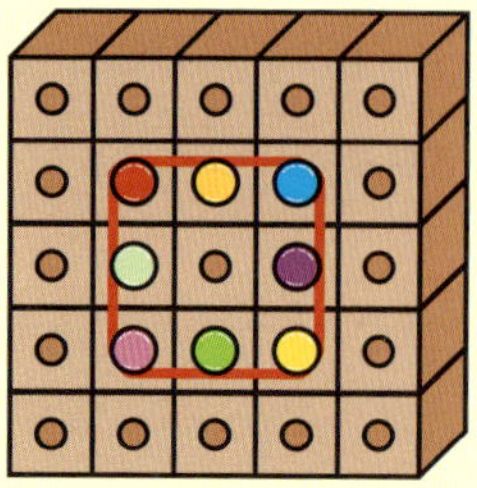

1 **How many right angles do these shapes have?**

a

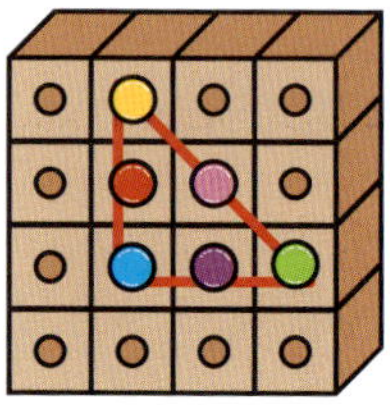

b

c

2 **Use a geo-board or spotty paper to make these shapes.**

a A quadrilateral with 1 right angle.

b A pentagon with 3 right angles.

c A hexagon with 2 right angles.

d A quadrilateral with 2 right angles.

3 **What is the least number of sides a shape must have if it has 2 right angles?**

4 **Use your geo-board to make each letter of your name. In each letter, count:**

a the number of right angles

b the number of acute angles

c the number of obtuse angles.

Points on the compass

The compass has four main directions:
north, south, east and west.
Between these directions are north-east, south-east, south-west and north-west.

1 **Find a map of your country. On the map, identify:**

a the city or town that is furthest to the north of your country

b the city or town that is furthest to the south

c a place east of where you live

d a place west of where you live.

2 **Use a compass. Stand so that you are facing north.**

a How does the compass tell you where north is?

b Through which angle must you turn to face east?

c From north, which angle must you turn to face south?

d Which directions are 90° away from south?

e Which directions are 90° away from north-west?

3 **Work out the final direction you are facing for each set of instructions.**

a Start by facing north. Turn 90° in a clockwise direction. Then turn 135° in the opposite direction.

b Start by facing south-east. Turn 180° in an anti-clockwise direction. Then turn another 90° in the same direction.

4 **Make up some instructions for a friend to follow. Ask them to work out their final direction.**

Clockwise and anti-clockwise

The hands of a clock always turn in the same direction so that they pass through the numbers on the clock face in order from 1 to 12.

This direction is called **clockwise**.

The opposite direction is called **anti-clockwise**.

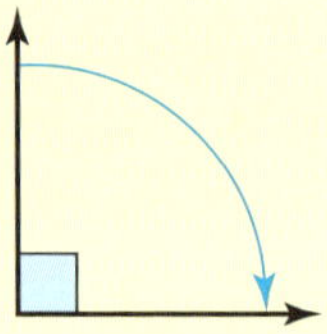

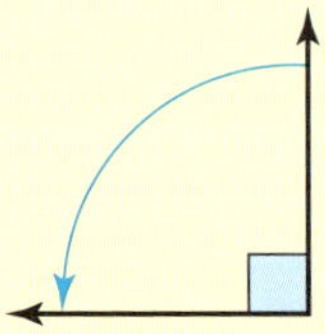

Play this game. Work in groups of five. One pupil calls out instructions using any of these directions:

clockwise, anti-clockwise, quarter-turn, half-turn, full turn, 90 degrees, 180 degrees.

Every time the 'caller' gives an instruction, the group must follow correctly. Anyone who gets the direction wrong must sit down. The winners are the last three people standing.

Here are some examples of directions:

- Walk clockwise in a circle.
- Walk anti-clockwise in a circle.
- Make a clockwise movement with your right hand.
- Turn 90 degrees to the right.
- Make a full turn, then take one step forward.
- Make a half-turn, then take two steps to the left.
- Make anti-clockwise circles with your head.

Make up any other directions that you wish!

you can use Workbook page 20

Identify and measure the turn

The pointer starts by pointing to north. The picture shows you which direction it moves to its end position.

The angle is 135°.

The direction is clockwise.

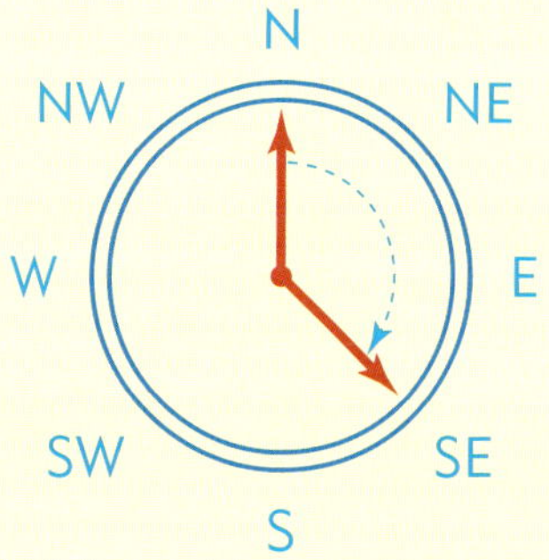

1 **For each turn of the pointer, measure the angle and identify the direction.**

a

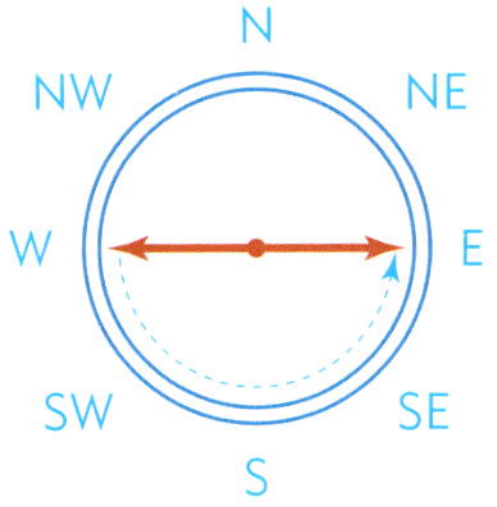

b

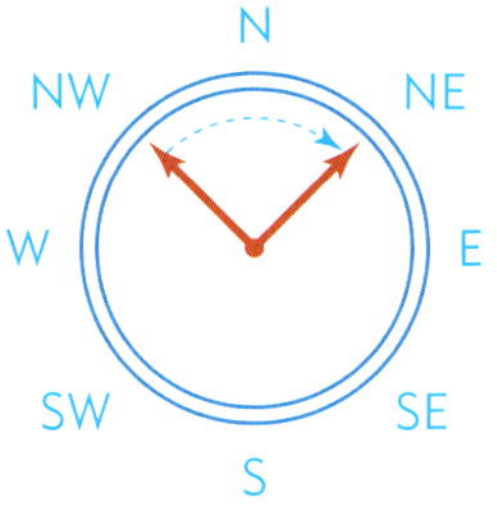

c

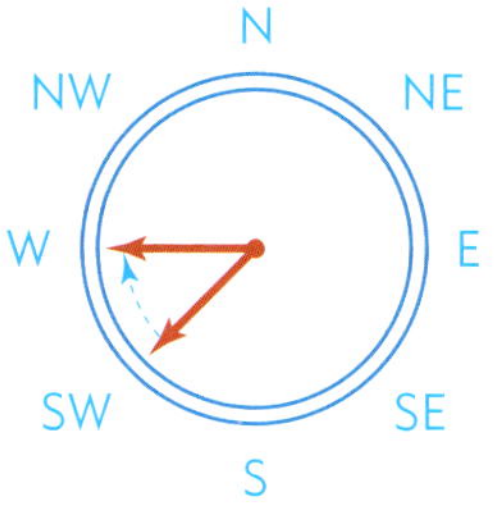

d

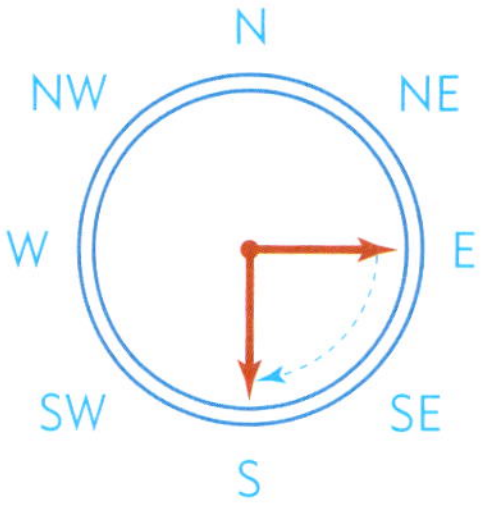

2 **Solve these problems.**

a I am facing south. I make a quarter turn clockwise. Where am I facing now?

b I am facing west. I make a half-turn anti-clockwise. Where am I facing now?

c I am facing south-west. I make a quarter turn clockwise and then a half-turn anti-clockwise. Where am I facing now?

3 **Make up similar direction problems for a friend to solve.**

you can use Workbook page 21

Reflections

Layla held up a triangle against a mirror.

The reflection showed the same triangle pointing in the opposite direction.

In maths, a **reflection** is a change in the position of a shape. It is also known as a 'flip', because the shape looks like it has been flipped over to the opposite direction.

1 **Use a small mirror and some cut-outs of polygons such as triangles and rectangles. Hold up each polygon to the mirror. Say what you notice about the reflections.**

2 **Use grid paper. Copy these shapes.**

Draw a reflection of each shape along the dotted line of symmetry.

a

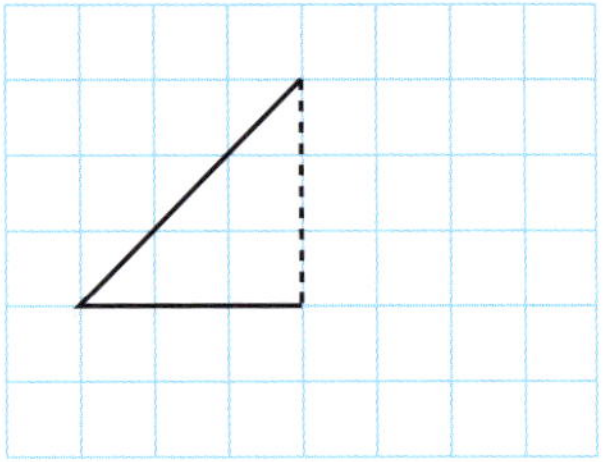

b

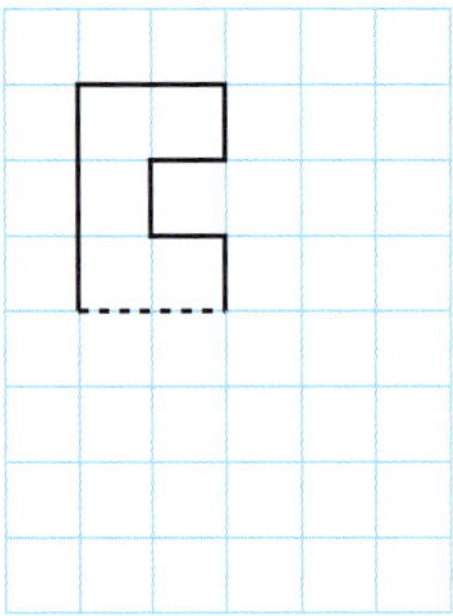

you can use Workbook page 22

Negative numbers

Have you ever seen numbers with a negative sign in front of them?

This elevator has floors below the ground floor.

If you count down from the second floor, the floors go down in this order:

2, 1, 0, –1, –2

Numbers that are less than 0 are called **negative numbers**.

1 **Copy each number line and complete the missing numbers.**

a –6 ___ –4 ___ ___ –1 0 1 2 ___ 4 ___ 6 7 8

b –25 –24 ___ ___ –21 –20 –19

c –150 –100 –50 ___ ___

d –60 ___ ___ ___ 20 40 ___ ___

e ___ ___ ___ 0 10 ___ 30

2 **Copy and fill in <, > or = between each pair of numbers.**

a 25 ___ –25 **b** –5 ___ –6 **c** 0 ___ –5

d –10 ___ –5 **e** –2 ___ –1 **f** –100 ___ –200

3 **Did you have any difficulty comparing the numbers in question 2? Why? Write a tip for comparing negative numbers.**

you can use Workbook page 23

Reading a thermometer

°C means 'degrees Celsius' or 'degrees Centigrade'.

Degrees are the units of measurement for heat.

0°C is the temperature at which water freezes (turns to ice). Negative numbers on a thermometer show us temperatures below freezing.

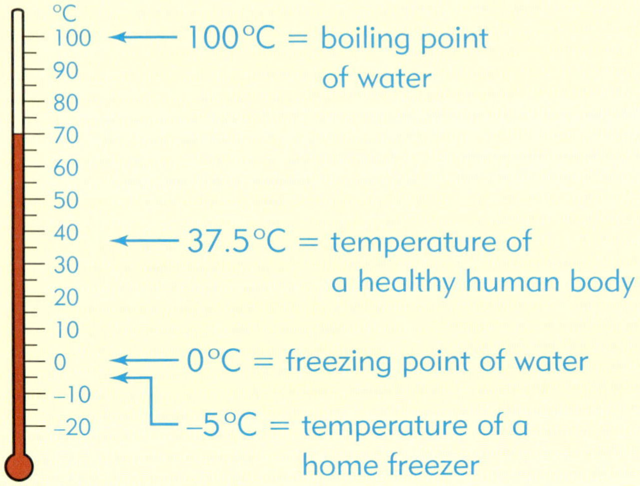

1 **Write the temperature shown on each thermometer.**

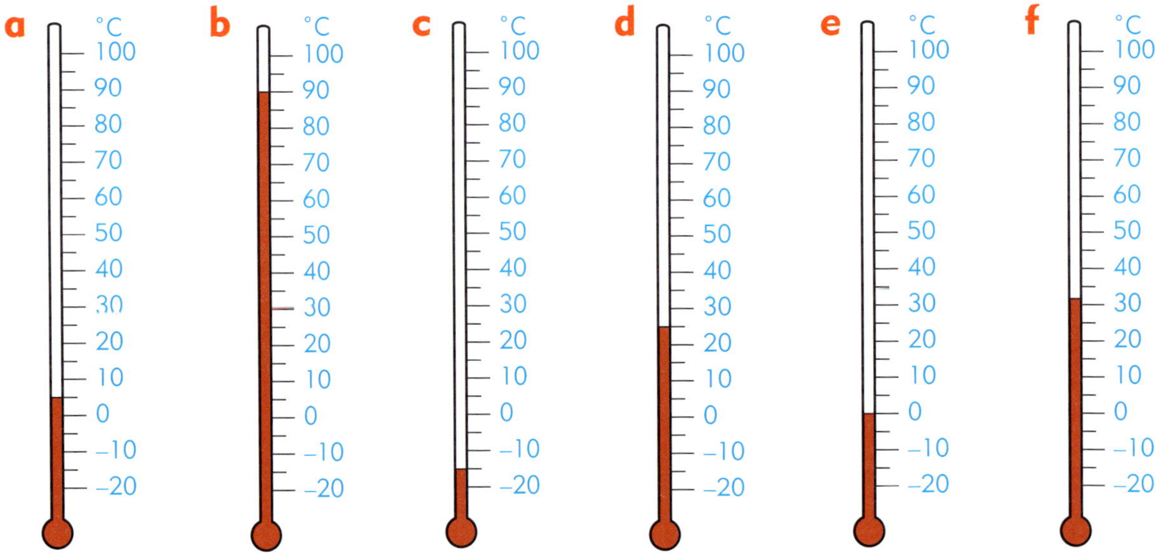

2 **Write the temperatures from question 1 in order from coldest to hottest.**

3 **Find out the temperatures of these things.**

a The oven temperature for baking a cake.

b The surface of Venus.

c A car engine when it is running.

One day in winter

When Wendy went to sleep one winter's night, it was –5°C. During the night, the temperature fell 10°C.

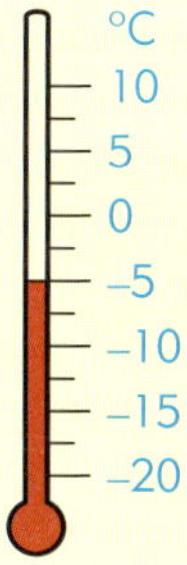

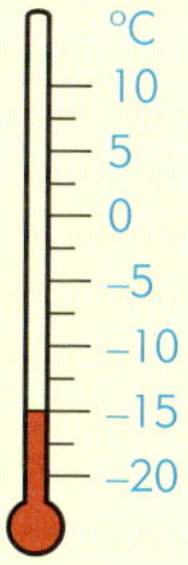

By noon the next day, the temperature had risen 20°C.

1 Copy and complete this chart about temperature changes. Estimate the time of day.

Starting temperature	Change	Temperature after change	Time of day
13°C	Rose 7°C		
8°C	Rose 5°C		
2°C	Fell 3°C		
–4°C	Fell 6°C		
–7°C	Fell 5°C		
–1°C	Rose 5°C		

2 Make your own temperature chart for a day. Take the temperature every hour.

3 Write down the warmest and coldest times of the day.

Assessment 1

1

a 7 + 5

b 6 + 9

c 5 + 4

d 11 + 8

e 20 – 8

f 30 – 10

g 27 – 9

h 42 – 5

i 45 ÷ 9

j 28 ÷ 4

k 45 ÷ 5

l 12 ÷ 4

m 7 × 8

n 6 × 6

o 4 × 9

p 3 × 8

2 **Rearrange each set of numerals to make as many three-digit numbers as you can. Then write the numbers in order from smallest to greatest.**

a

b

c

d

3 **Write the name of each polygon.**

a

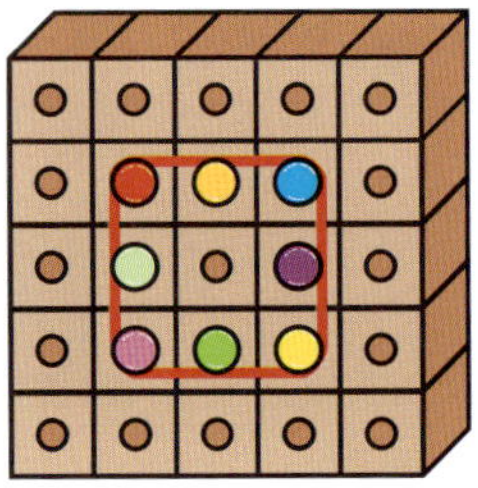

b,c

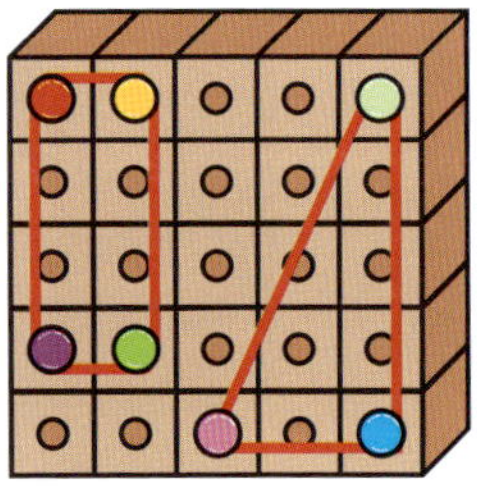

d

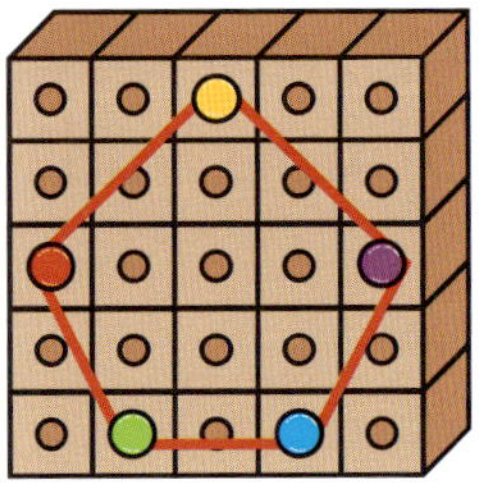

4 **Write 'true' or 'false' for each statement.**

a The net of a cone must have two flat circular faces.

b The net of a cube has six identical square faces.

c The net of a cuboid has six rectangular faces that are not necessarily the same size.

d The net of a pyramid can never have more than four triangular faces.

5 **Round off to the nearest ten.**

a 11 pins

b 175 people

c 218 computers

d 397 badges

6 **Divide. Give remainders if necessary.**

a $100 \div 10$ b $18 \div 5$

c $28 \div 6$ d $35 \div 4$

e $64 \div 7$ f $39 \div 10$

7 **Multiply.**

a 2×100

b 6×100

c 10×100

8 **Copy and complete the table.**

Angle	In degrees	Turn
	90	
Straight line / two right angles		
Three right angles		Three-quarter turn
		Full turn

9 **Write the correct direction.**

a I am facing north. I turn 90° clockwise. Which direction am I facing now?

b I am facing west. I turn 90° anti-clockwise then 180° clockwise. Which direction am I facing now?

10 **Copy and complete each number sequence.**

a 10, 5, 0, ___, ___, ___

b 8, 6, 4, ___, ___, –2, ___, ___, ___

Getting data organised

A teacher asked pupils in his class which two pieces of fruit they would like to take with them on the class picnic. To help him buy the fruit, he made this tally chart.

Fruit	Tally
Apples	卌 卌 卌 IIII
Pears	卌 卌 III
Oranges	卌 卌 IIII
Bananas	卌 卌
Peaches	卌 IIII
Mangos	卌 II

1 How many of each of these fruits would the teacher need to buy?

a apples **b** pears **c** oranges
d bananas **e** peaches **f** mangos

2 Remember each pupil in the class was allowed to choose two fruits. How many pupils are there in the class altogether?

3 Imagine your class is going on a picnic. Find out which two pieces of fruit each pupil would like to take. (You can choose a different variety of fruit if you wish.) Make a tally chart.

Frequency tables

The **frequency** of a value is the number of times it occurs.

1 **A class of 20 pupils got the following marks out of 10 for an assignment:**

7	6	6	7	5	8	10	9	9	7
7	7	6	5	7	10	8	7	6	7

a Copy this table.

Mark	Tally	Frequency
5		
6		
7		
8		
9		
10		

b Complete the second column of the table by tallying how frequently each mark occurs.

c Write the total in the third column.

2 **Find out the ages of pupils in your class in years. Draw a simple frequency table to show your results.**

3 **Do a survey of what time each pupil in your class goes to bed, rounded off to the nearest quarter-hour. Draw a simple frequency table to show your results.**

you can use Workbook page 24

A typical day

Maria drew a graph of how she spent one school day.

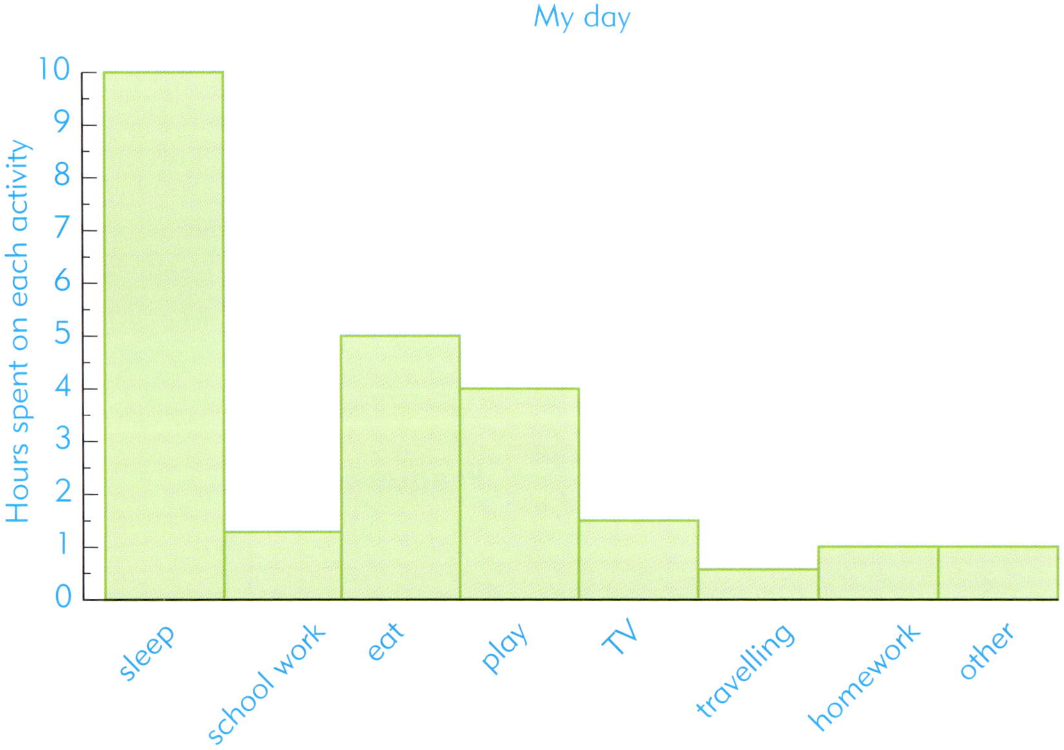

1 Answer the questions.

a How long did she spend eating?

b How long did she choose to watch TV?

c How much time did her homework and school work take up?

d What did she spend the longest time doing?

e What did she spend the shortest time doing?

2 Make your own chart showing how long you spend on different activities during the day.

Who uses the shop?

A newsagent wanted to find out how many people used his shop in the school holidays in case he needed to order extra stock.

He counted the people who came into his shop between 12:30 p.m. and 1:30 p.m. Here is a graph showing the results of his survey.

1 How many of each of these groups were there?

a girls **b** boys **c** women

d men **e** babies

2 How many people visited the shop altogether?

3 Do you think the graph would look different if the newsagent collected the information during the school term?

4 Do you think the graph gives the newsagent clear information about whether or not to order new stock? Give reasons for your answer.

Check the temperature

Rajesh took the temperature every hour during the school day. Here is a graph showing his results.

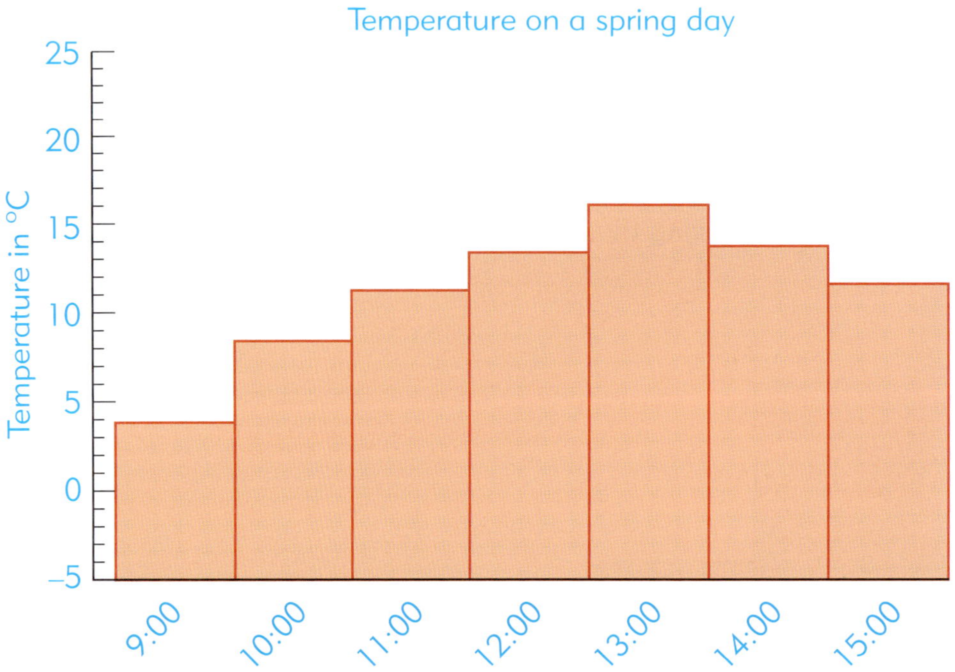

1 Answer these questions.

a What was the temperature at 11 a.m.?

b What was the coolest part of the day?

c Was it warmer at 12 noon or 3 p.m.?

d What do you think the temperature might have been at 4 p.m.?

---

2 Check the temperature at hourly intervals throughout one day. Make your own bar chart to show the information.

3 Check the temperature at 10 a.m. for three consecutive days. How much does it vary?

Hundreds, tens and units

6 hundreds → 625 ← 5 units

↑

2 tens

625 = 600 + 20 + 5

This is called **expanded form**.

1 **Count and work out the number. Write each number using expanded form.**

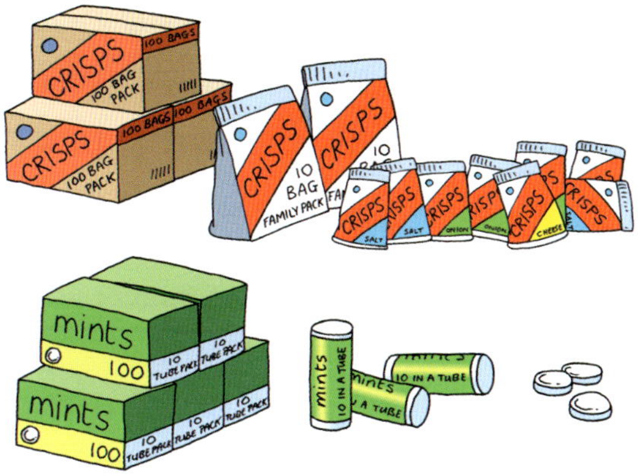

a How many bags of crisps altogether?

b How many mints altogether?

2 **Write the numbers shown by these labels.**

a

100
100 10 1
100
10 10 1 1
100
10 10 1

b

100 10 10 1
10 10 10 10 1 1
10 10 10 1 1

c

100 1 1 1
1
100 1 1 1

d

100 100 100 1
100 100 10 10
100 100 10

3 **Write these in expanded form.**

a 613	**b** 226	**c** 879	**d** 547
e 984	**f** 732	**g** 461	**h** 358

you can use Workbook pages 25–7

Zig-zag number track

0 1 2 3 4 5 6 7 8 9 10 11 12 13 14 15 16 17 18 19 20

21 22 23 24 25

1 Use the number track to count in these different ways. Write each number you jump onto.

a Start at zero. How many jumps of five to reach 65?

b Start at zero. Jump in sevens to 84.

26 27 28 29 30 31 32 33 34 35 36 37 38 39 40 41 42 43 44 45 46

47 48 49 50 51

c Start at 90. Jump back in sixes. How many jumps to reach zero?

d Start at 96. Jump back in eights. How many jumps to reach zero?

e Start at 99. Jump back in nines. How many jumps to reach zero?

f Start at 80. Jump back in fives. How many jumps to zero?

52 53 54 55 56 57 58 59 60 61 62 63 64 65 66 67 68 69 70 71 72

73 74 75 76 77

2 Design your own number track to 100. Use different colours to show jumps of five, jumps of six, and so on.

78 79 80 81 82 83 84 85 86 87 88 89 90 91 92 93 94 95 96 97 98

99 100

3 Teams of children picked strawberries. After 5 minutes, each team stopped and shared the strawberries out. Which team got the best share for each person?

In team A, 5 children picked 66 strawberries.
In team B, 6 children picked 72 strawberries.
In team C, 4 children picked 50 strawberries.
In team D, 7 children picked 87 strawberries.

Make your own problems

Kyra picked three cards. They were 4, 3 and 6.

She made all the possible multiplications she could.

They were:

$43 \times 6 = 258$
$46 \times 3 = 138$
$36 \times 4 = 144$
$63 \times 4 = 252$
$64 \times 3 = 192$
$34 \times 6 = 204$

She also tried:

$4 \times 3 \times 6$
$3 \times 4 \times 6$
$6 \times 4 \times 3$
$6 \times 3 \times 4$

But she found they all made 72.

Use these cards to do the same.

1 1 5 7

2 4 9 3

3 8 0 6

4 2 5 4

5 **Make your own numeral cards from 0 to 9. Put them face down. Turn them over three at a time. Make all the possible multiplications.**

What happens after 999?

1 Start at 999. Add or count on these numbers. Write the answers.

a 1	**b** 3	**c** 7	**d** 11
e 22	**f** 68	**g** 96	**h** 125

2 Gemma started with 1235 in her calculator. She wanted to get to 2546.

She added 1000. She added another 300.

Use your calculator and write the next steps she might take to get to 2546.

3 Use your calculator and write the steps you would take to get from:

a 2615 to 4273

b 1965 to 2964

c 5125 to 9999

d 2345 to 3456

e 8765 to 4321

Working with 1000s

We can also write the number 4765 using expanded form:

$4000 + 700 + 60 + 5 = 4765$

1 **Write the value of the underlined digit in each number.**

a $5\underline{2}40$ **b** $1\underline{0}98$ **c** $\underline{1}609$

d $\underline{3}182$ **e** $80\underline{5}6$ **f** $\underline{7}484$

g $\underline{6}179$ **h** $2\underline{1}47$ **i** $97\underline{6}2$

2 **Now write each of the numbers from question 1 using expanded form.**

3 **Write each of these numbers using numerals.**

a two thousand, eight hundred and forty-three

b six thousand and sixty-five

c eight thousand and fifteen

d seven thousand, two hundred and twenty

e four thousand and four

---

4 **Use a newspaper. Cut out some examples of four-digit numbers. Write them in different ways:**

a as words

b using expanded form.

you can use Workbook page 28

1 Write these numbers in order, from least to greatest.

a	6125	1372	5827	3150	6324
b	2895	3199	1596	2250	1826
c	5643	4291	6126	5242	4871
d	9875	8982	9645	8777	7958
e	6708	7729	5936	6599	6821
f	1986	2135	1520	2448	1992

2 Draw this number line in your book.

This shows approximately where **2555** is on the number line.

Mark these numbers approximately on your number line.

a 3125 **b** 4287 **c** 4980

d 5217 **e** 1856 **f** 2799

you can use Workbook page 29

Which is best?

These instruments are all used for weighing.

1 kg 575 g can be written as 1.575 kg

1 **Write down what you would use to weigh the following objects. Also write down whether the result would be in kg, g or kg and g.**

a your best friend

b a pencil

c a large bag of potatoes

d a small bag of rice

e a paperback book

f a brick

If possible use real examples to check your answers.

---

2 **Write down the answers to the questions in your book.**

a How much do you weigh?

b What would you be worth if your weight was measured in 50c coins?

c What would you be worth if your weight was measured in $1 coins?

(Hint: You will need to weigh a real 50c coin and a real $1 coin. You may wish to use a calculator to help with the working out.)

you can use Workbook page 30

Measuring height and weight

You will need:

- bathroom scales
- a measuring tape
- grid paper.

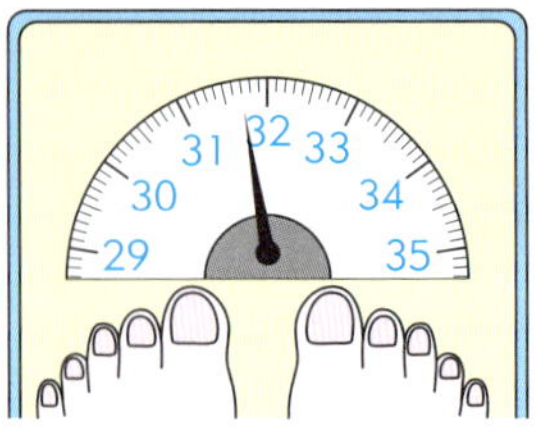

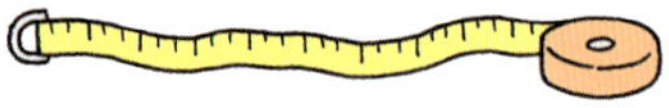

1 **Work in groups of ten children. Use a table like the one on the right to record the information.**

a Measure each person's weight using the bathroom scales.

b Measure each person's height using the measuring tape.

Name	Weight	Height

2 **Now plot co-ordinates to show the relationship between weight and height.**

Use grid paper and label the axes to show weight and height as shown. Then plot the co-ordinates using weight as your *x* co-ordinate and height as your *y* co-ordinate.

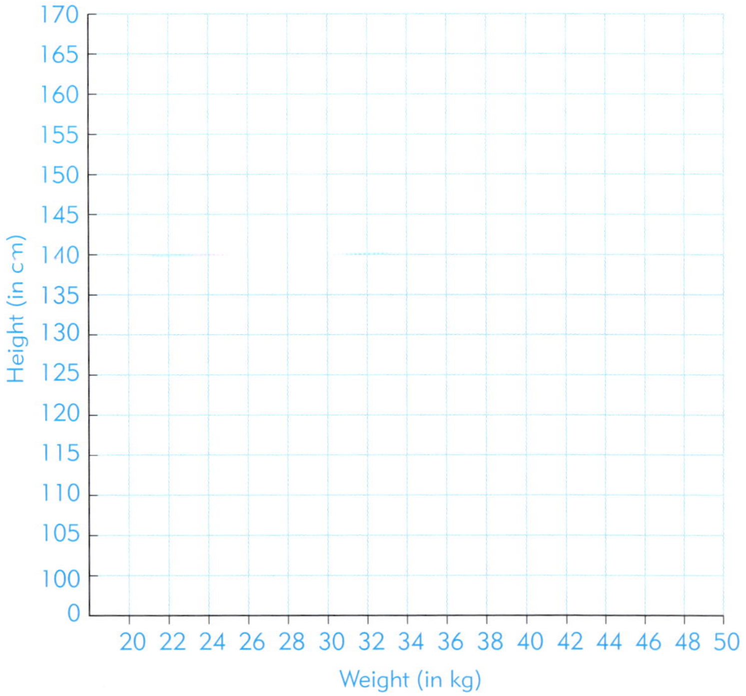

3 **Discuss what you notice about the co-ordinates.**

you can use Workbook page 31

Make your own clock

You will need:

- cardboard
- split pins or wire
- marker pens
- a pair of scissors.

1 Follow these steps.

a Draw a large clock face on the cardboard.

Draw the numbers in the correct positions around the clock face.

It helps to start with 12, 3, 6 and 9 so that you can get the positions correct.

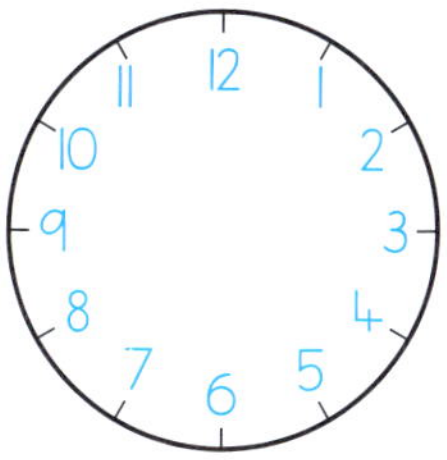

b Cut out two hands: one long, one short. These will be the minute hand and the hour hand.

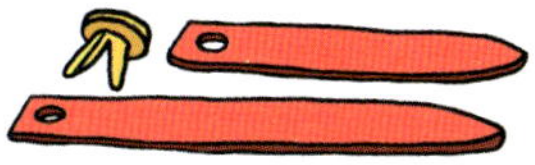

c Make a small hole at one end of each hand, and at the centre of your clock face.

Use split pins (or a piece of wire) to attach the hands to your clock face.

2 Now you can use your clock face to show different times.

a twelve o'clock
b half past seven
c five to eleven
d five to nine
e quarter to six
f twenty past eight

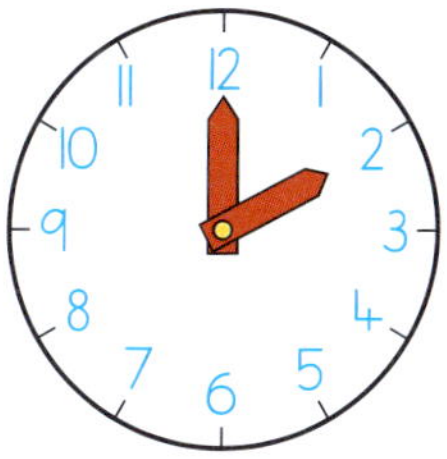

Analogue time

A clock face with numbers and hands is known as an **analogue clock**. The minute hand makes a full turn around the clock face every hour, but the hour hand makes a full turn every 12 hours.

1 **Which number on the clock face does the long hand (the minute hand) point to when it is the following times?**

a half past the hour

b quarter to the hour

c quarter past the hour

d 25 minutes past the hour

e 10 minutes past the hour

f five minutes before the hour

2 **Write each time in words.**

a

b

c

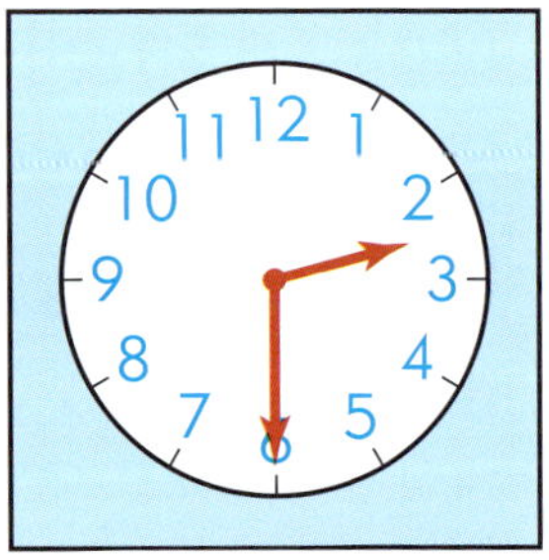

d

e

f

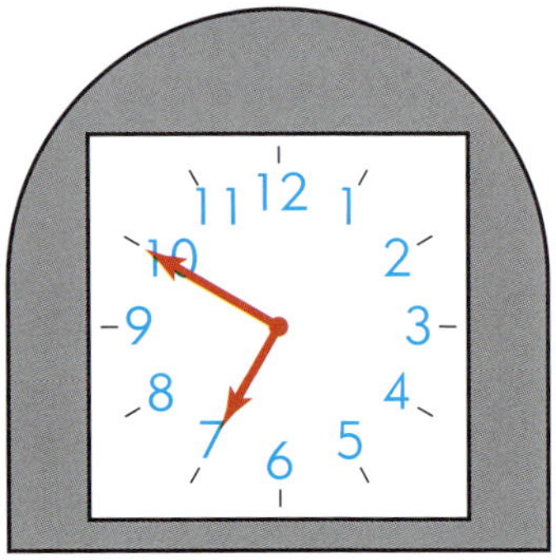

Digital time

A **digital clock** only uses numbers to tell the time. For example:

The 'a.m.' means 'before noon'. Times from midnight to midday are a.m. times. Times from midday to midnight are p.m. times.

11:00 a.m.
(hours) (minutes)

Two hours later, the time will be 1:00 p.m. or 1 o'clock in the afternoon.

Some digital clocks use 24-hour notation, which does not need a.m. and p.m.

In 24-hour notation, we write 11:00 a.m. like this: 11:00.

Two hours later, the time will be 13:00.

1 **Copy and complete the table.**

Time in words	**a.m./p.m. time**	**24-hour notation**	**1 hour later (24-hour notation)**
Five o'clock in the afternoon	5:00 p.m.		18:00
Half past three in the morning		03:30	
Seven o'clock in the evening			
Twelve o'clock at night		00:00	
Quarter to one at lunchtime			13:45
Twenty to eight in the morning	7:40 a.m.		
Twenty-five past eleven at night			
Ten to five in the morning			

2 **Now show each of the times above on the clock face you made.**

you can use workbook page 32

How long did it take?

Clare began the cross-country running race at 09:30. She finished 4 h 21 min later. What time did she finish?

Starting time: 9 h and 30 min
Time taken (elapsed time): 4 h and 21 min
Finishing time: 13 h and 51 min
She finished at 13:51.

Clare's friend began the race at 09:45 and finished at 14:57. How long did he spend running?

Finishing time: 14 h and 57 min
Starting time: 9 h and 45 min
Elapsed time: 5 h and 12 min
He was running for 5 h 12 min.

1 **Here is a chart of starting times, elapsed times and finishing times for four runners. Some of the times are missing. Copy the chart and fill in the missing times.**

Runner	Starting time	Elapsed time	Finishing time
A	08:20	5 h 10 min	
B	10:05	6 h 2 min	
C	09:13		16:20
D	08:27		15:50

2 **The race officials started work at 08:15. They worked for 10 h 30 min. What time did they finish work?**

3 **Think of an activity, like making a tables square, walking once around the playground, or reading a page of your book. Make a chart like the one above. Time yourself and your friends.**

you can use Workbook page 33

Take a commercial break

1 **Most commercial breaks on television last $3\frac{1}{2}$ minutes. Look at the list of advertisements. How long will each commercial break last?**

Product	**Length of ad in seconds**
Opal Gti	30
Dunlot Tyres	40
Delmonde Fruit	10
Waterline Showers	30
Supermart sale	30
Vogaphone summer special	40
Big Cone ice cream	30
Bonds Skin Cream	20
Cornflakes	30
Superclean washing liquid	20
Royal Tea	30
Charity appeal	40
Everlast holiday resorts	30

a Waterline Showers, Bonds Skin cream, Royal Tea, Opal Gti, Big Cone ice cream, Vogaphone summer special, Dunlot Tyres.

b Cornflakes, Delmonde Fruit, Superclean washing liquid, Charity appeal, Supermart sale, Dunlot Tyres, Everlast holiday resorts.

c Use the list to make up your own commercial break lasting exactly $3\frac{1}{2}$ minutes. Write the advertisements and their times.

2 **Using modelling clay or paper, make a boat that will float on water for at least 10 seconds. Estimate, then measure, the time it takes from collecting the materials to when the boat first floats. Working with a friend, compare your times with your estimates.**

Races and records

1 **This table shows the results of a men's 400 m hurdles race.**

Name	**Time in seconds**
Keith Young (UK)	48.1
John Masamba (Uganda)	47.8
Michael Lewis (USA)	47.6
Boris Burghardt (Germany)	48.7
Ralph Bell (USA)	47.7
Trevor Williamson (USA)	47.1

a Put the race times in order from slowest to fastest.

b Who would have won the gold, silver and bronze medals?

c Who finished in fifth place?

d Who finished between Michael Lewis and Keith Young?

e Who took 1.1 seconds longer than Michael Lewis?

You will need:

- sheets of paper
- a stopwatch that can time to $\frac{1}{10}$ of a second.

2 **With a partner, time how long it takes an A4 piece of paper to float to the ground. One person holds the paper horizontally 2 m above the ground. (Stand on a chair if necessary.) The other person times the fall of the piece of paper with a stopwatch. Do this five times. Record your results. Then try tissue paper, tracing paper and card. Compare your results.**

Athletics records

Women

Event	Time	Set by	Date
100 m	10.49	Florence Griffith-Joyner (USA)	1988
200 m	21.34	Florence Griffith-Joyner (USA)	1988
400 m	47.60	Marita Koch (Germany)	1985
800 m	1:53.28	Jarmila Kratochvílová (Czech Republic)	1983
1500 m	3:50.46	Yunxia Qu (China)	1993
10 000 m	29:31.78	Wang Junxia (China)	1993

Men

Event	Time	Set by	Date
100 m	9.58	Usain Bolt (Jamaica)	2009
200 m	19.19	Usain Bolt (Jamaica)	2009
400 m	43.18	Michael Johnson (USA)	1999
800 m	1:41.11	Wilson Kipketer (Denmark)	1997
1500 m	3:26.00	Hicham El Guerrouj (Morocco)	1998
10 000 m	26:17.53	Kenenisa Bekele (Ethiopia)	2005

1 How much faster is the men's record for 100 m than the women's record?

2 Does it take twice as long to run 400 m as 200 m? Check the record times to find out.

3 How much longer does it take the fastest women to run 1500 m than 800 m? Round off to the nearest minute.

4 If Michael Johnson could run the 800 m in his 400 m time, would he break Wilson Kipketer's record?

5 How long do you think it takes each of these athletes to run 50 m?

a Florence Griffith-Joyner **b** Usain Bolt

Pictogram

Look at the pictogram and answer the questions.

1 Which was the most popular flavour?

2 Which two flavours were equally popular?

3 How many more vanilla cones were sold than strawberry?

4 How many more chocolate cones were sold than mint?

5 Do you think the graph shows the exact number of ice cream cones sold? Give a reason for your answer.

6 How could a graph like this help someone running an ice cream shop?

Estimating

Sometimes, before we count an exact number, we can guess the number. This is called **estimating**. We can also estimate the answers to problems by rounding off the amounts before we calculate.

$\approx$ means 'equals approximately'.

$$29 + 32 \approx 30 + 30$$
$$\approx 60$$

$$\begin{array}{r} 29 \\ +\ 32 \\ \hline 61 \\ \hline \end{array}$$

1 Estimate, then count:

a the number of books on one shelf in your classroom or library

b the number of items in your suitcase or satchel

c the number of words in the box at the top of this page

d the number of pictures on one of your classroom walls.

2 Round off to estimate. Then calculate the accurate answer.

a 87 + 94 **b** 143 + 67 **c** 58 + 263

d 485 + 99 **e** 54 + 128 **f** 32 + 576

3 Estimate the total for each table's bill.

Table 1
8 × spring rolls
2 × soup
1 × noodles
1 × spicy fish

Table 2
2 × soup
2 × chicken stir fry
3 × spicy fish
1 × fried rice

you can use Workbook page 34

Fruit and nut problems

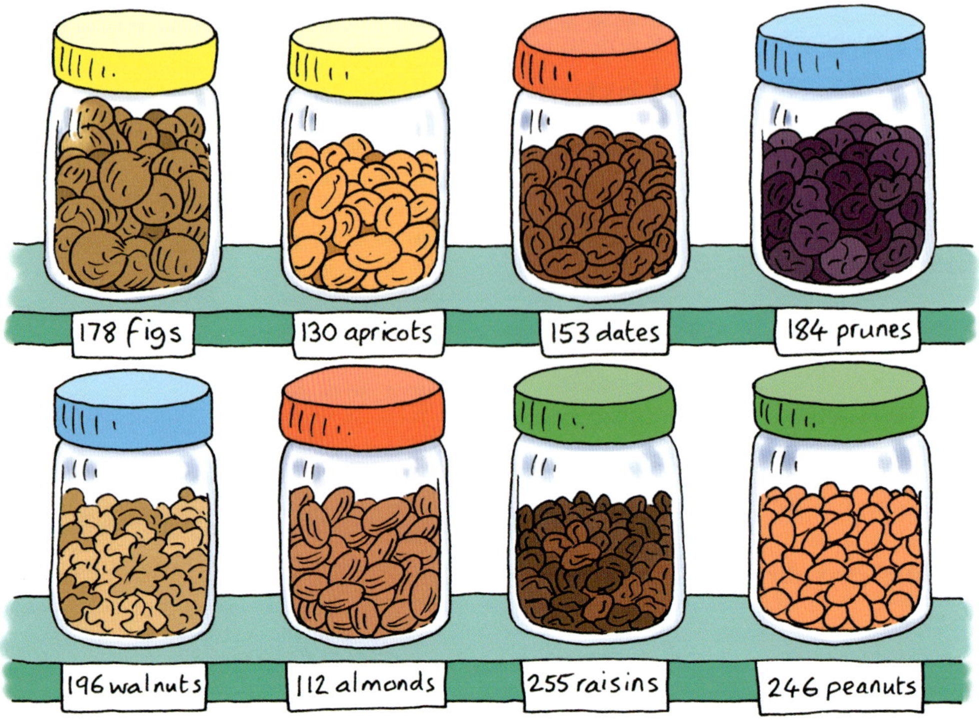

1 **Use the numbers of fruits and nuts to calculate the following.**

a How many figs and prunes are there altogether?

b How many nuts are not peanuts?

c How many apricots and figs are there altogether?

d How many nuts are there altogether?

e How many dried fruits are there altogether?

2 **Use the numbers in the boxes. Write ten different additions with answers less than 1000.**

246	353	537
883	902	364
518	672	826

you can use Workbook page 35

Rounding up, rounding down

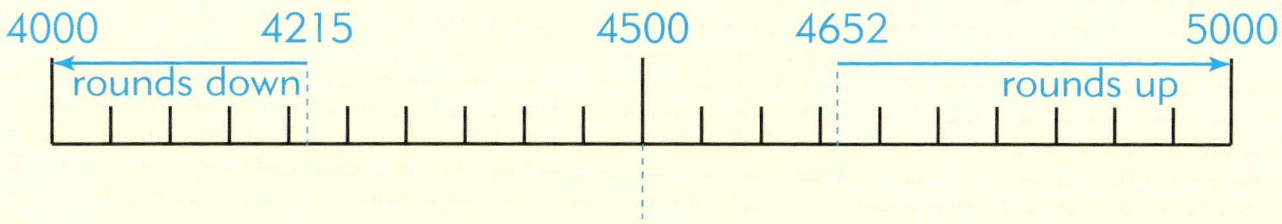

Numbers from 4001 to 4499 round **down** to 4000.

Numbers from 4500 to 4999 round **up** to 5000.

1 **Round these numbers up to 5000 or down to 4000.**

a 4170 **b** 4753 **c** 4500 **d** 4265
e 4851 **f** 4359 **g** 4672 **h** 4499
i 4900 **j** 4820 **k** 4065 **l** 4577

2 **Here are some more four-digit numbers. Round up or down to the nearest thousand. Draw a number line if it will help you.**

a 2449 **b** 6921 **c** 8689 **d** 3162
e 5863 **f** 7500 **g** 4425 **h** 9267
i 3318 **j** 1282 **k** 4099 **l** 8989

3 **These numbers have been rounded to the nearest thousand. What is the smallest, and largest, number they could have been?**

a 2000 **b** 5000 **c** 3000 **d** 7000

4 **What patterns do you notice in your answers to question 3?**

you can use Workbook page 36

Rounding money

Sometimes it is helpful to round prices to the nearest dollar.

For example, \$21.99 rounds up to \$22.

Sometimes it helps to work out costs if you round to the nearest \$10. For example, \$22 rounds down to \$20.

Rounding can also help you to estimate the answer to a sum.

3192 + 5763 can be rounded to:

$3000 + 6000 \approx 9000$

The true answer is 8955, which rounds to 9000.

1 **For each price in the picture above, round it off to the nearest dollar and nearest \$10.**

2 **Estimate the answers to these, then check with a calculator.**

a 3126 + 5255

b 1763 + 7042

c 4927 + 2846

d 5162 + 4825

e 1208 + 2540

f 3018 + 3819

g 1282 + 7982

h 4811 + 3995

Subtraction on a number line

Sometimes drawing a number line can help you to find the difference between two numbers.

For example, Anna drew this number line to help solve the problem 423 – 378:

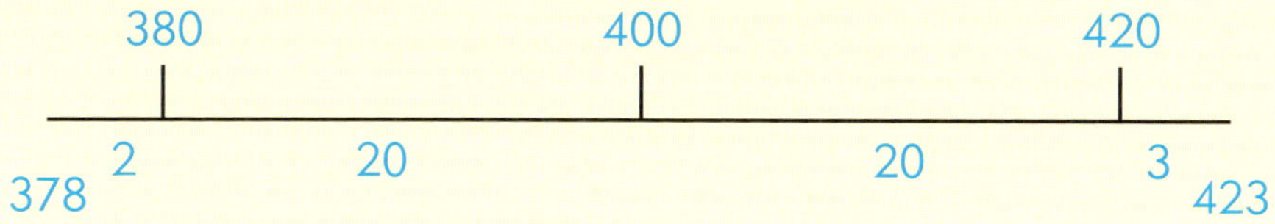

She added on from 378:

2 + 20 + 20 + 3

Anne got the answer 45.

1 **Try drawing number lines to find these differences.**

a 692 – 545 **b** 321 – 267 **c** 816 – 797 **d** 433 – 312

e 924 – 799 **f** 211 – 158 **g** 572 – 451 **h** 734 – 686

2 **I spilled coffee on this list of price changes. Write out my new list showing the price changes.**

Item	Old price	New price	Price rise
Fridge	$325	$359	
Washer/drier	$427		$125
Cooker	$645		$254
Microwave	$197	$215	
Dishwasher		$385	$98

Coded subtractions

In this code, each letter of the alphabet stands for a digit from 0 to 9:

A	B	C	D	E	F	G	H	I	J	K	L	M	N	O	P	Q	R	S	T	U	V	W	X	Y	Z
0	1	2	3	4	5	6	7	8	9	0	1	2	3	4	5	6	7	8	9	0	1	2	3	4	5

1 Solve these problems using the code.

a Subtract **ABC** from **DEF**. Write the number.

b What number is the difference between **POD** and **PEA**?

c Write a code for the answer to 471 – 289.

d What number is the difference between **HIM** and **HER**?

e Subtract **LMN** from **HIJ**. Write the number.

f Write a code for the answer to 689 – 302.

g What number is the difference between **FISH** and **CAT**?

h Subtract **WXY** from **STU**. Write the number.

i Write a code for the answer to 842 – 377.

j What number is the difference between **CAR** and **BUS**?

2 Make up your own coded subtractions.

3 In these subtractions, some of the digits are missing. Write them out with all the digits.

a 439 – 1___6 = 31___

b 5___7 – 263 = ___74

c ___25 – 532 = 1___3

d 86___ – ___45 = 623

you can use Workbook pages 37–39

Assessment 2

1 **This tally chart shows the number of different types of book we counted in my classroom. Answer the questions about the tally chart below.**

Reading books	卌 卌 卌 卌 IIII
Exercise books	卌 卌 卌 卌 I
Textbooks	卌 卌 III
Dictionaries and reference	卌 IIII
Other	卌 卌 I

a What kinds of book do we have the most of?

b What kinds of book do we have the least of?

c How many more exercise books than textbooks are in our class?

d How many books are in the 'dictionaries and reference' and 'other' sections altogether?

e How many books did we count altogether?

2 **Draw a bar chart showing the information from the tally chart.**

3 **Write these numbers using expanded form.**

a 198 **b** 2473 **c** 602 **d** 5039

4 **Use this number line to help you round off the numbers below to the nearest thousand.**

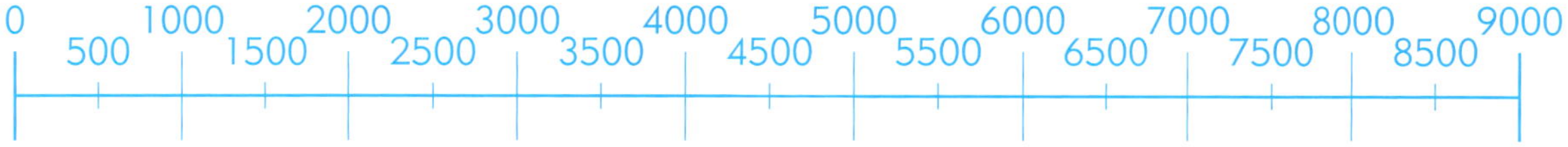

a 7291 **b** 6080 **c** 4325 **d** 8450

Assessment 2

5 **Write whether you would weigh each item in kilograms or grams.**

a

a cupcake

b

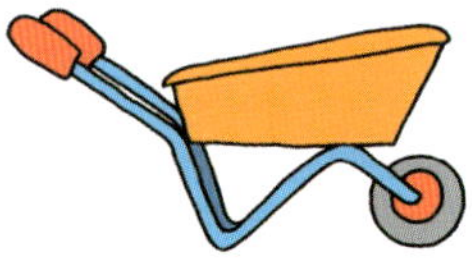

a wheelbarrow

c

a mobile phone

d

a slice of bread

e

a box of potatoes

f

a box of books

6 **Write the time shown on each clock in words and also in digital notation.**

a

in the morning

b

at night

c

in the afternoon

d

at night

Number patterning

Cells increase by splitting.

You can use counters to represent cells.

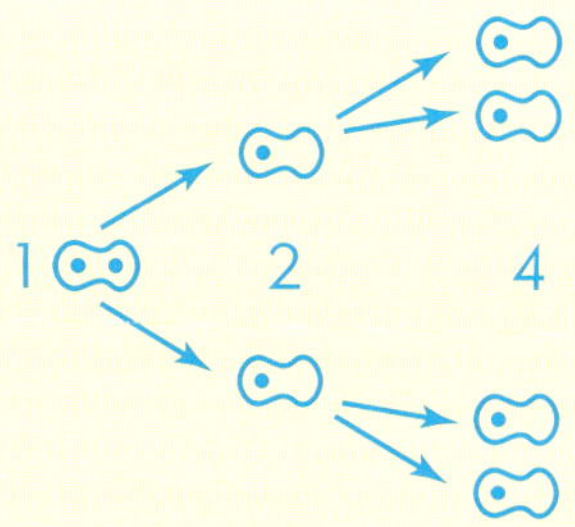

1 **Start with one counter.**

a Make a pattern to show how the cells continue to split.

b Draw the pattern and write the number of cells after each split. Carry on drawing as far as 6 splits.

c How many cells are there after 5 splits?

d How many cells would there be after 7 splits?

e How many cells would there be after 10 splits?

f What do you notice about the pattern?

2 **Paul used 1 cm mosaic tiles to make picture frames.**

He wrote down how many tiles he used in each one. His pattern was 10, 14, 18. He then measured the perimeter of each frame with a ruler. He found the measurements made a different pattern: 14 cm, 18 cm, 22 cm.

a Continue his pattern of picture frames until you have made six of them.

b Write down the numbers in your series of tiles and perimeters.

c How do the patterns grow?

you can use workbook page 40

Finding patterns in the 100 square

A 100 square with the numbers arranged like this has many patterns.

1	2	3	4	5	6	7	8	9	10
11	12	13	14	15	16	17	18	19	20
21	22	23	24	25	26	27	28	29	30
31	32	33	34	35	36	37	38	39	40
41	42	43	44	45	46	47	48	49	50
51	52	53	54	55	56	57	58	59	60
61	62	63	64	65	66	67	68	69	70
71	72	73	74	75	76	77	78	79	80
81	82	83	84	85	86	87	88	89	90
91	22	93	94	95	96	97	98	99	100

1 Describe the pattern of:

a each row **b** each column **c** each diagonal

2 There are also hidden patterns in the square.

Look at the numbers 30, 31 and 32.

Add their digits: $3 + 0 = 3$ $3 + 1 = 4$ $3 + 2 = 5$

What do you notice about the pattern of their sums?

3 Investigate the digital sums of the numbers in:

a a row **b** a column **c** a diagonal

4 Find some L-shaped numbers in the square. Add the digits of each number in the L-shape. Describe the pattern you find.

24		
34		
44	45	46

5 What other patterns can you find in the hundred square?

You might like to try 'crosses' and 'steps'.

	65	
74	75	76
	85	

77		
87	88	
97	98	99

Number prisms and pyramids

1 In this triangular prism each end face is worth 25. Each side face is worth 36. What do all the faces add up to? Don't forget the hidden ones.

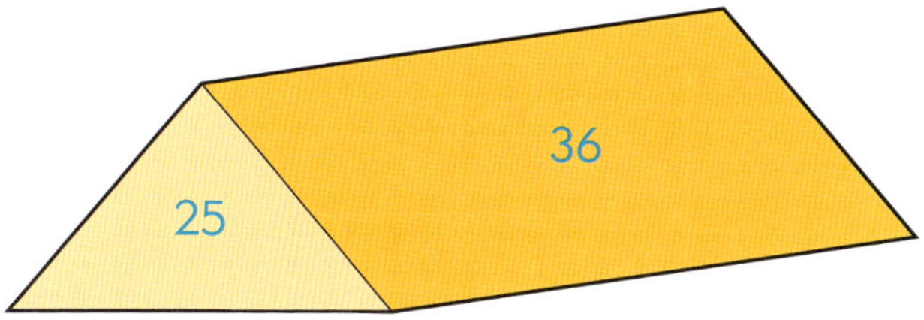

2 Add all the faces in each of these shapes.

a

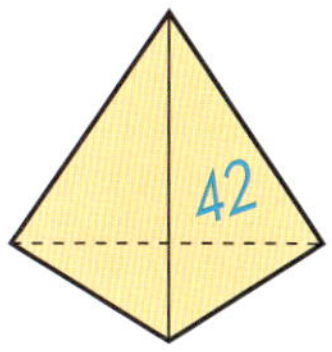

tetrahedron

b

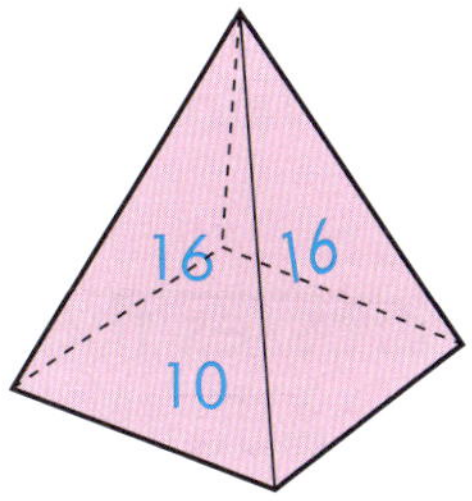

square-based pyramid

c

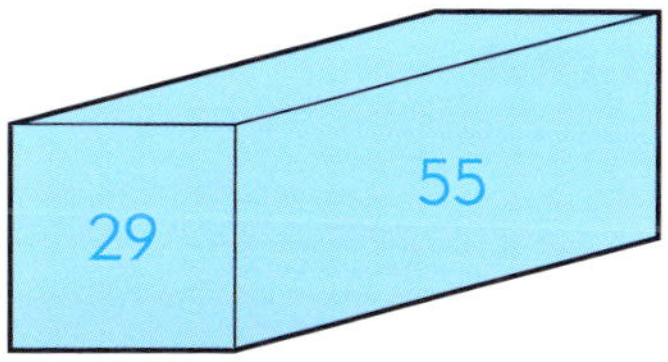

cuboid

d

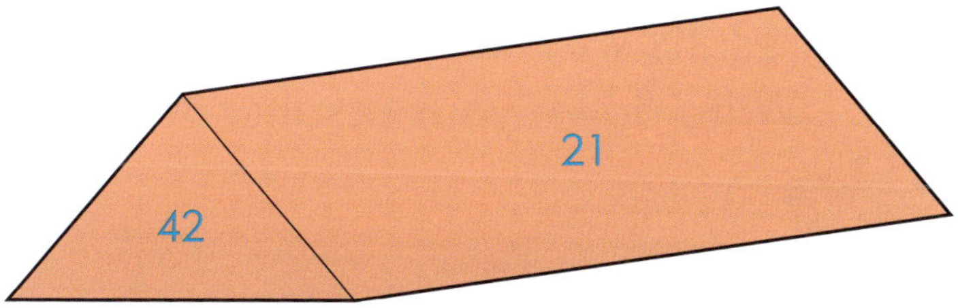

triangular prism

3 Look at this number maze. You can use + or – between the numbers in this maze.

Write routes that finish with these totals.

a 79 **b** 12

c 9 **d** 27

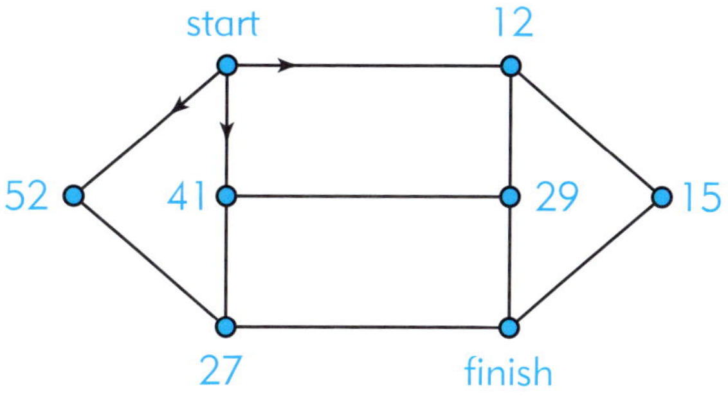

Crosses in the multiplication square

You will need a tables square.

X	1	2	3	4	5	6	7	8	9	10
1	1	2	3	4	5	6	7	8	9	10
2	2	4	6	8	10	12	14	16	18	20
3	3	6	9	12	15	18	21	24	27	30
4	4	8	12	16	20	24	28	32	36	40
5	5	10	15	20	25	30	35	40	45	50
6	6	12	18	24	30	36	42	48	54	60
7	7	14	21	28	35	42	49	56	63	70
8	8	16	24	32	40	48	56	64	72	80
9	9	18	27	36	45	54	63	72	81	90
10	10	20	30	40	50	60	70	80	90	100

1 Look at the first cross marked on the table square, with 8 in the top position.

a Add together the numbers at the top and bottom of the cross, then the numbers at the left and right of the cross. What do you notice?

b Do the same with the other shaded cross. What do you notice?

c Mark some crosses the same size on your own tables square. Add the numbers in the same way. Write down your results. What do you notice?

d Do you think you will get the same kinds of results with larger crosses? Try some to find out. Write down your results. Were you right?

2 In this cross the average of 21 and 27 is 24. The average of 16 and 32 is 24. Note that 24 is the centre number. Try this with other crosses. Write down the averages.

14	21	28
16	24	32
18	27	36

If you add together a set of figures, then divide the total by the number of figures you added, the result is called the **average**.

For example, $3 + 5 = 8$ and $8 \div 2 = 4$.
The average of 3 and 5 is 4.

$4 + 7 + 10 = 21$. As $21 \div 3 = 7$,
the average of 4, 7 and 10 is 7.

you can use Workbook pages 41–6

Frequency diagrams

Remember: You will need to decide on a scale for your frequency diagram. It needs to be clear enough to read easily. It must also fit the paper.

Ella did a traffic survey to find out which was the most popular car in her area. Here are her results.

Mercedes	𝍸 III	Ford	𝍸 𝍸 𝍸 𝍸 𝍸 II
Nissan	𝍸 II	Vauxhall	𝍸 𝍸 𝍸 II
BMW	𝍸	VW	𝍸 I
Suzuki	I	Skoda	𝍸 𝍸 𝍸 IIII
Fiat	III	Mazda	I
Mitsubishi	I	Citröen	II
Saab	I	Peugeot	𝍸 II
Toyota	IIII	Renault	III
Audi	I	Volvo	𝍸 IIII
Kia	I	Honda	IIII
Jaguar	I	Chrysler	

1 **Use this tally chart to draw a frequency diagram of her results.**

2 **List the five most popular cars, according to her research.**

3 **Which makes of car are most popular in your area? Do a survey to find out. Draw a frequency diagram to show your results.**

A database: big cats

A **database** is a chart.

It shows information set out in 'fields'.

In this database about big cats, the fields are in the column at the side.

They are 'length', 'continent', 'prey', 'colour', and so on.

	Lion	**Tiger**	**Leopard**	**Ocelot**

Length	2.75 m	3 m	2.25 m	1.25 m
Continent	Africa	Asia	Asia, Africa	South America
Main prey	wildebeest	deer	baboons, deer	small mammals
Colour	pale brown (tawny)	orange and black	yellow and black	grey, fawn black
Markings	none	stripes	spots	spots and stripes
Habitat	plains	jungle	plains	forest and jungle

Using a database

1 **Answer the following questions by using the 'big cats' database on the previous page.**

a What do lions eat?

b How long is an ocelot?

c On which continent do tigers live?

d What sort of markings do leopards have?

e Which big cats do baboons avoid?

f Which cats live on the plains?

g Which is the longest big cat?

h Which big cat lives in South America?

2 **Find out more about other big cats – for example, the panther, the lynx, the cheetah, etc.**

Make your own database using the files and fields on the previous page. Add any more fields you are interested in – for example, life span, number of kittens in a litter, whether they are endangered or not.

3 **Do you have a hobby, collection or special interest? Design your own database – for example, if you collect coins from different countries, you could write down the country, the currency, the value and what is shown on them.**

Fractions

1 part of 4 is shaded:

therefore, $\frac{1}{4}$ or one quarter.

3 parts out of 4 are not shaded:

therefore, $\frac{3}{4}$ or three quarters.

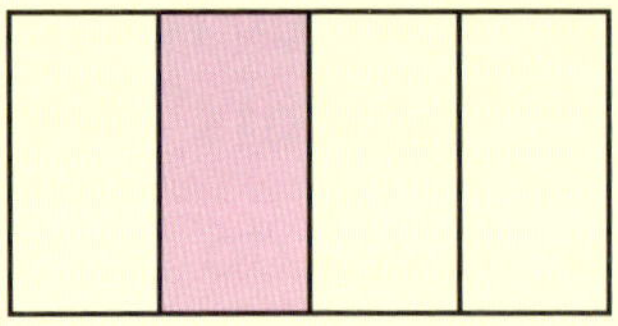

Remember: A **fraction** is a part of a whole number or set.

You will need:

- squared paper
- scissors
- coloured pencils.

1 **Cut out strips and colour them to show these fractions.**

a $\frac{1}{2}$ **b** $\frac{3}{4}$ **c** $\frac{2}{3}$ **d** $\frac{5}{6}$

e $\frac{4}{5}$ **f** $\frac{7}{8}$ **g** $\frac{3}{10}$ **h** $\frac{8}{9}$

2 **Cut a piece of squared paper 6 × 6. How many different fractions can you show by colouring?**

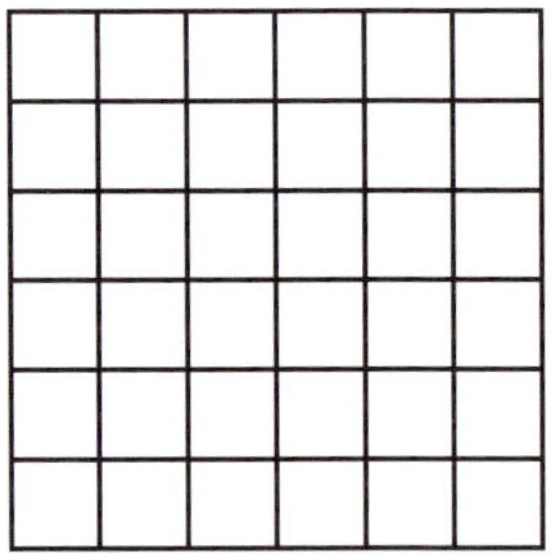

3 **Here is one way to colour one quarter of a square:**

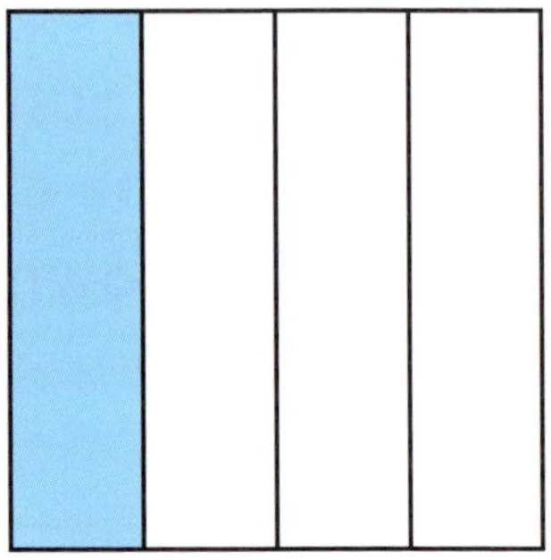

a Find as many other ways as you can to colour one quarter of a square.

b Choose a different fraction. Choose a different shape. Show your fraction in as many different ways as you can.

you can use Workbook pages 47–49

Fractions of solid shapes

This picture shows a cube made up of smaller cubes.

Use the picture or make your own cube to help you answer the questions.

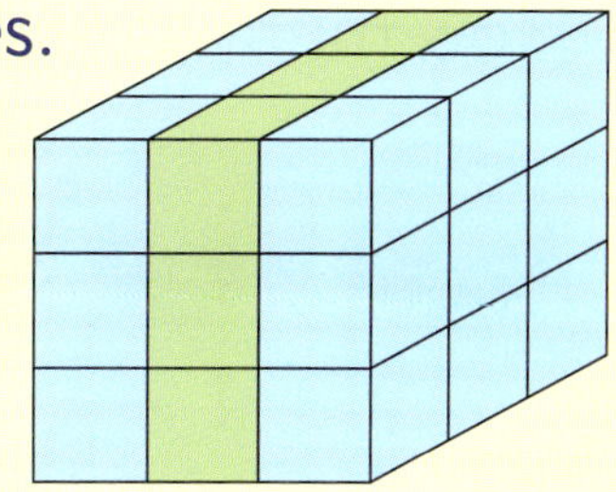

1 Use your cube to calculate the following.

a How many cubes are there altogether?

b If you took one third of the cubes away, how many would be left?

c Draw $\frac{1}{9}$ of the cubes.

d $\frac{4}{9}$ of the cubes are in one pile. The rest are in another pile. How many cubes are there in each pile?

2 These cubes have been put together to make a cuboid.

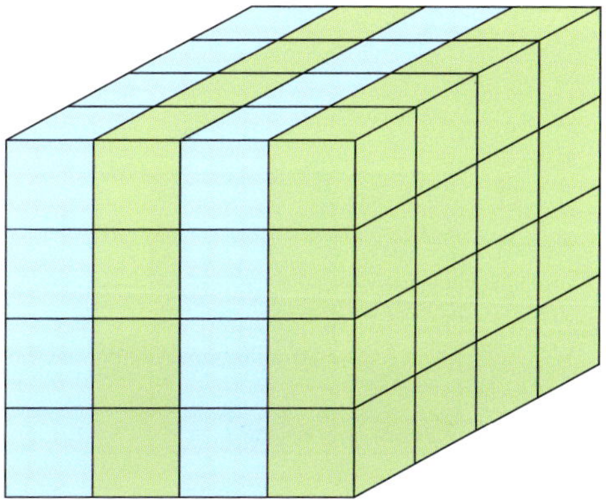

a How many cubes are there altogether?

b What fraction of the cubes are green?

c Draw $\frac{1}{8}$ of the blue cubes.

d Add together $\frac{1}{4}$ of the blue cubes and $\frac{1}{4}$ of the green cubes. How many cubes do you have?

e Put $\frac{1}{6}$ of the green cubes in a row. Put $\frac{1}{8}$ of the blue cubes in a row. Which row has more cubes?

3 Make or draw your own cuboid. Try a different size or use three colours for the bricks.

4 Make up some problems about your cuboid for a friend.

Mixed numbers and fractions

How many burgers are there?

$1 + 1 + \frac{1}{2}$

$2\frac{1}{2}$

$\frac{2}{2} + \frac{2}{2} + \frac{1}{2}$

$\frac{5}{2}$

$2\frac{1}{2}$ is a **mixed number**.

$\frac{5}{2}$ is a fraction greater than 1.

1 How much is coloured? Write the answers in two ways.

a

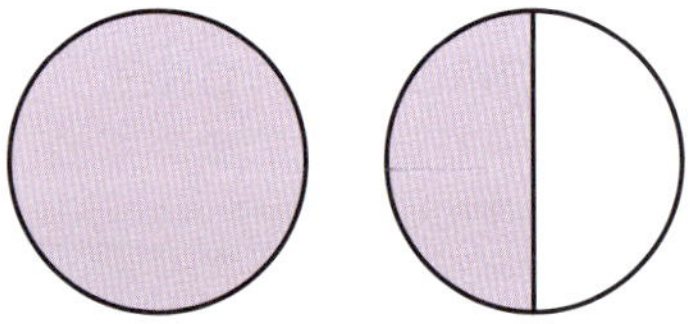

b

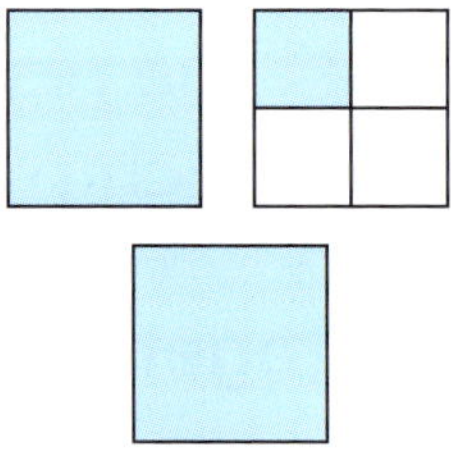

c

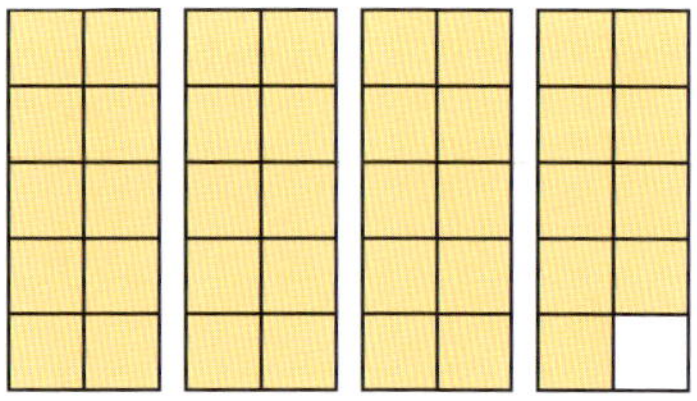

d

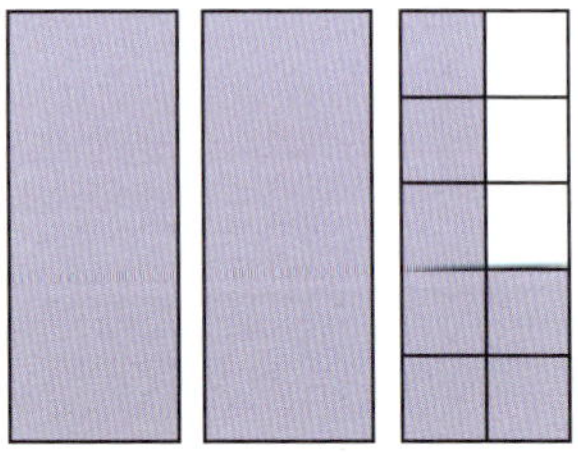

e

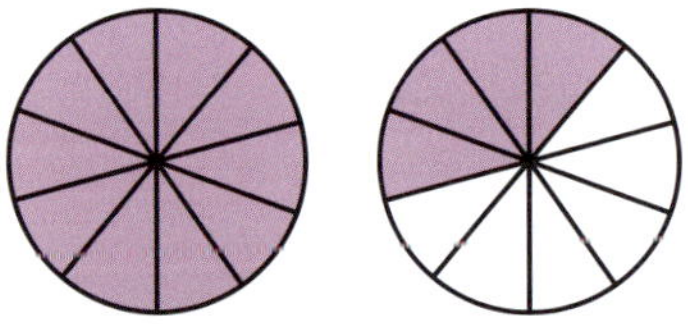

f

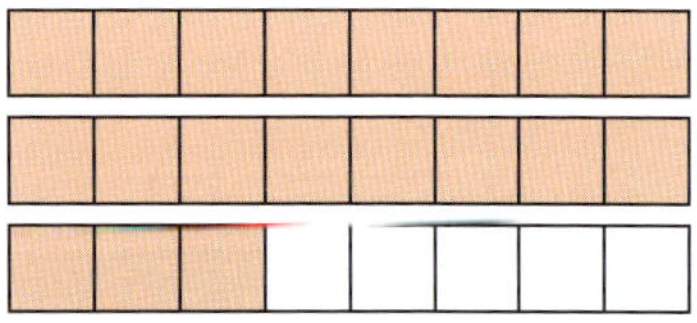

g

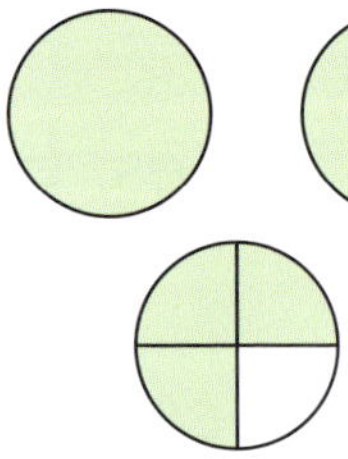

h

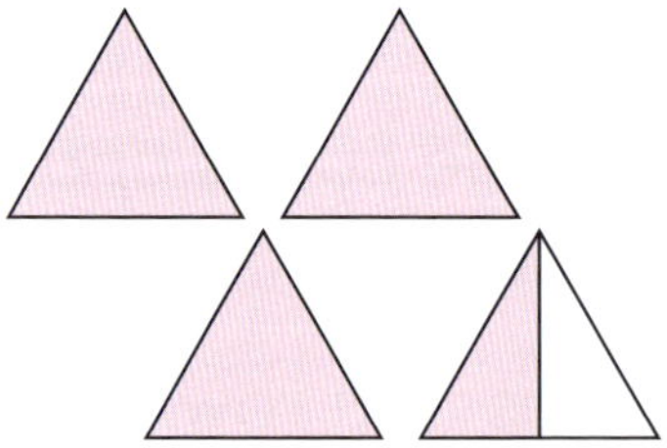

i

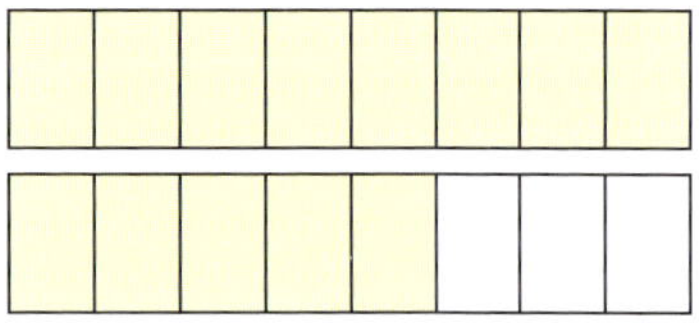

2 Draw your own pictures to show these mixed numbers and fractions.

a $2\frac{1}{2}$ **b** $\frac{5}{4}$ **c** $1\frac{2}{3}$

d $3\frac{1}{8}$ **e** $\frac{11}{10}$ **f** $\frac{12}{5}$

1 Solve these problems. Draw pictures to help you.

a The Stone family ordered 2 pizzas. Each pizza was cut into eighths. The family ate 15 pieces. What fraction of the pizzas did they eat?

b Steve picked some tomatoes from his garden. When he cut them into quarters he had 12 pieces. How many tomatoes did he pick?

c Four people ordered 5 chapattis with their curry. How much did each person get if they were shared exactly?

d Three cakes were cut up for the party. There were 15 guests and each had a fair share. What fraction was each cake cut into?

2 Write the mixed number.

a If  = 1,

then 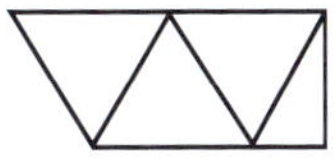 is?

b If  = 1,

then 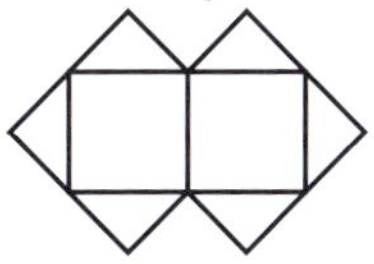 is?

c If 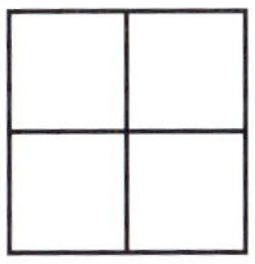 = 1,

then 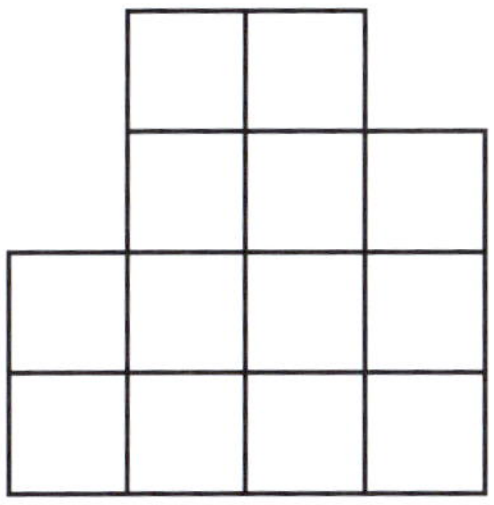 is?

d If 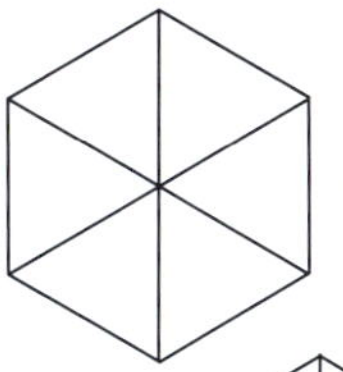 = 1,

then 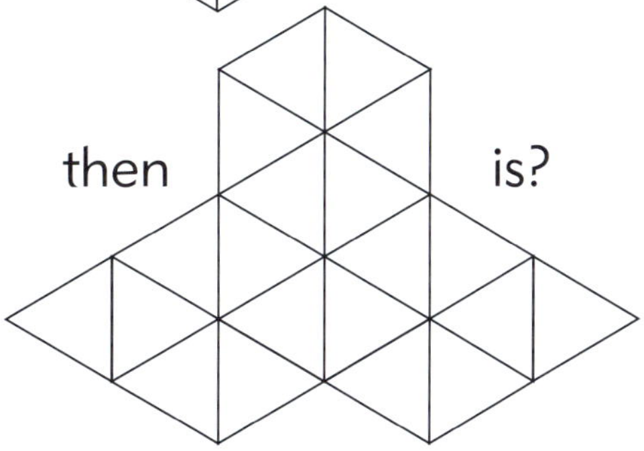 is?

3 Make up some similar puzzles for a friend to try.

Horizontal and vertical lines

Horizontal lines are level, flat lines parallel to the horizon.

The black line is horizontal.

Vertical lines are upright and at right angles to the horizon.

The red line is vertical.

1 Say which lines in the picture are horizontal, and which are vertical.

2 Draw your own picture showing horizontal and vertical lines.

Use one colour for horizontal and another for vertical.

3 Look around the classroom. Find six horizontal and six vertical lines. Write down where they are.

Treasure hunt

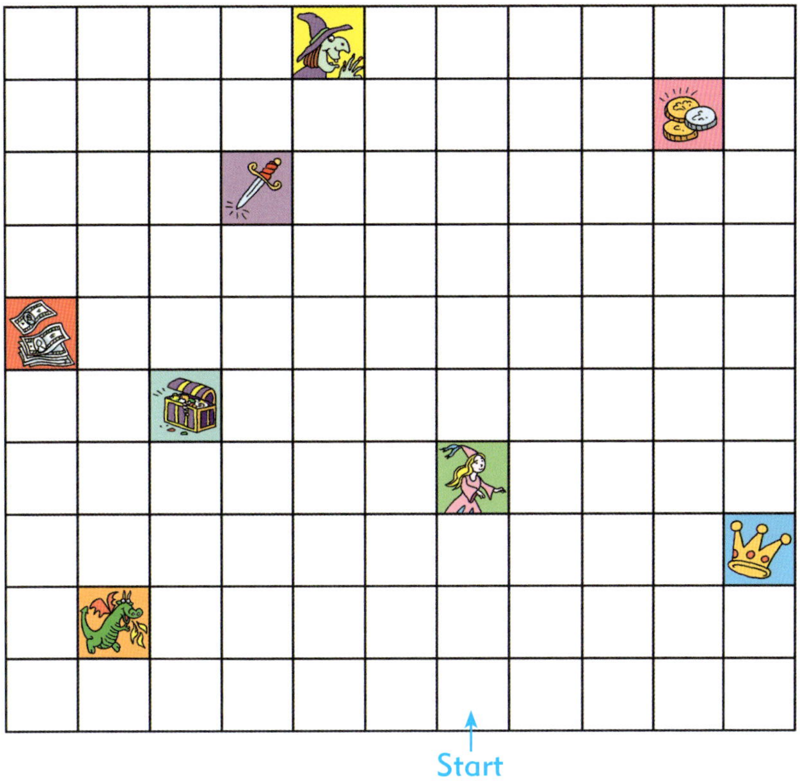

1 **Use the grid above. Solve each problem.**

a From the start move vertically 5 spaces up. Move horizontally 4 spaces left. What do you find?

b From the start, move horizontally 5 spaces to the left. Move vertically 1 space up. What do you find?

c Start at the sword. Give directions to move horizontally and vertically to go and kill the dragon.

d Start from the witch. Give directions to reach the crown in 2 moves.

2 **Copy this grid. Add some more treasures and troubles.**

Make up some questions for your friends.

you can use Workbook pages 50–2

Tenths

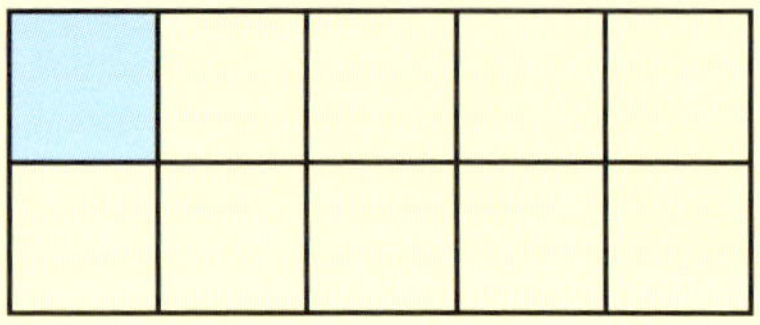

100	10	1	$\frac{1}{10}$
		0	• 1

The shaded block shows one tenth or $\frac{1}{10}$

We can write this in another way: 0.1

The unshaded blocks are $\frac{9}{10}$ or 0.9

The dot is a decimal point that comes after the numeral in the units' place.

1 **Count in tenths from 0 to 1.**

Write out the numbers as decimals.

2 **Look at the three sums below. Explain any patterns that you notice.**

$$99 + 1 = 100$$
$$9 + 1 = 10$$
$$0.9 + 0.1 = 1$$

\$1 = 100c or 10 × 10c

Each 10c is 0.1 of \$1. We can put an extra 0 after the decimal point like this:

\$1.50 = one dollar and fifty cents
= one and five tenths

3 **Write these amounts using decimal notation.**

a Two dollars and two tenths of a dollar.

b Six dollars and nine tenths of a dollar.

c Ten dollars and one tenths of a dollar.

you can use Workbook page 53

Decimal pictures

This picture shows a decimal abacus.

There are 2 tens → 20
3 units → 3
6 tenths → .6

It shows 23.6

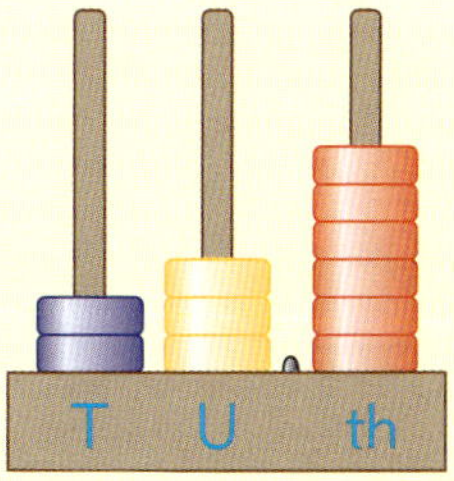

1 **Write the numbers these abacus pictures show.**

a

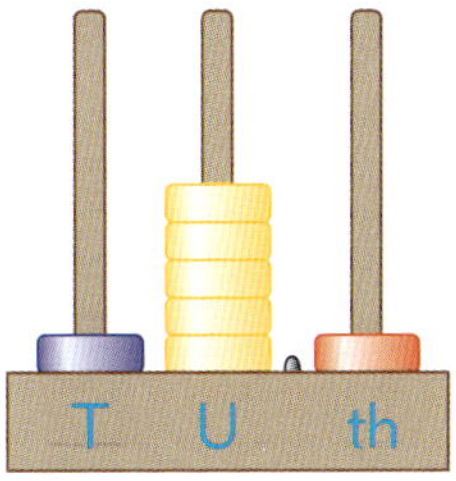

b

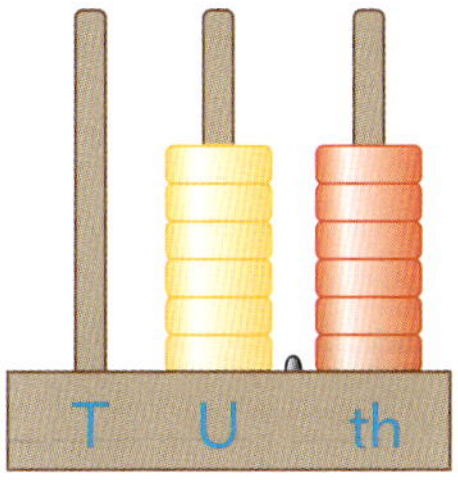

c

d

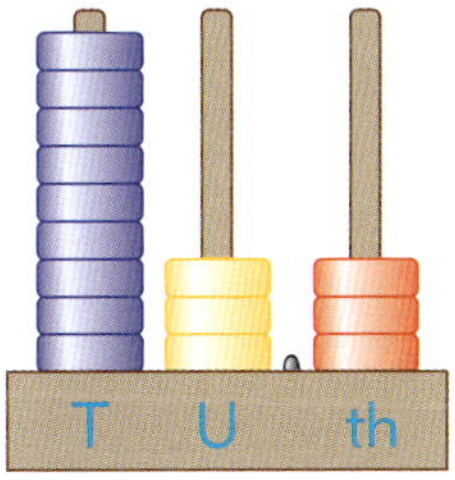

e

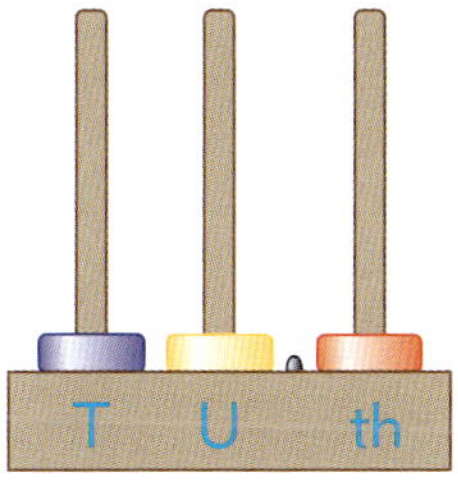

f

2 **Draw abacus pictures to show these numbers.**

a 62.4 **b** 5.5 **c** 83.0 **d** 20.8

3 **You will need an abacus or a drawing of an abacus and some beads.**

a Using only three beads, how many different decimal numbers can you make? Here is one possibility.

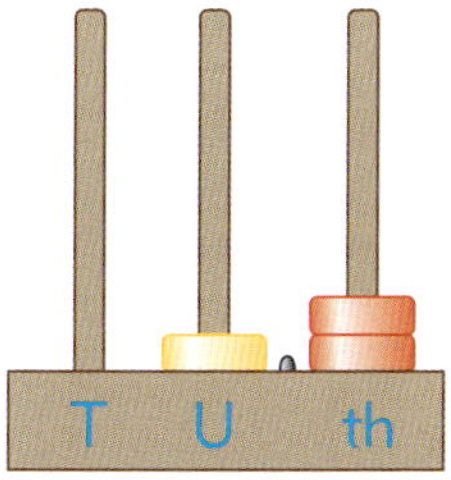

b Try again using four beads, five beads, and so on.

Fruit punches and cocktails

Anita made an orange and pineapple punch for the party. She mixed 1.5 litres of pineapple juice with 2.5 litres of orange juice.

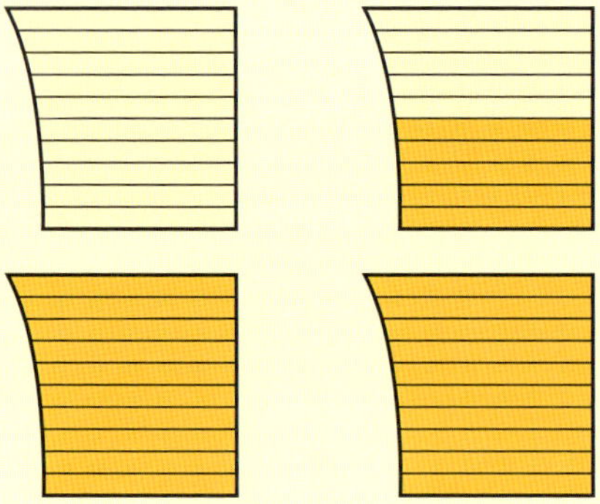

1.5l + 2.5l

She made 4.0l of punch.

How much punch would you get from these recipes?

1 **Apple and blackcurrant punch:**
1.5l apple juice, 0.5l blackcurrant juice, 1.5l lemonade

2 **Mixed fruit cocktail:**
0.3l grape juice, 0.2l pineapple juice, 0.4l apple juice, 0.5l mineral water

3 **Grape and ginger soda:**
0.7l grape juice, 0.5l ginger ale, 1.2l soda water

4 **Citrus ice cream fizzer:**
0.6l orange juice, 0.4l lime juice, 0.8l lemon squash, 1.5l lemonade, 0.4l vanilla ice cream

5 **Do you know the recipe for a punch or cocktail? If not, make one up, using your favourite flavours, to make 4 litres.**

Counting in tenths

0 0.5 1 1.5 2 2.5 3 3.5 4 4.5 5

1 Use the number line.

a Count in tenths from 0.7 to 1.6
Write all the numbers.

b Count back in tenths from 2 to 1.1
Write all the numbers.

2 Now do these in the same way.

a 2.5 to 4.3 **b** 0.6 to 1.9 **c** 3.8 to 2.6

d 4.0 to 2.8 **e** 2.9 to 3.3 **f** 2.1 to 0.9

3 Use your calculator.

a Write a list of numbers from 1 to 25. Use your calculator to divide each number by 10. Write the new numbers beside those you started with. Can you see the pattern? Write about it.

b Try some more numbers.

you can use Workbook page 54

Greatest and least

1 **Order these decimal numbers from greatest to least.**

a 6.8, 5.9, 7.1

b 15.3, 20.5, 9.7, 19.7

c 86.8, 87.9, 86.5, 87.1

d 31.4, 59.0, 39.1, 45.2, 51.1

2 **Order these decimal numbers from least to greatest.**

a 9.8, 4.3, 11.1, 7.4

b 15.3, 9.4, 12.8, 10.0

c 43.3, 39.1, 36.8, 41.0, 36.2

d 19.9, 18.7, 19.1, 18.3, 19.6

---

3 **Make your own decimal numbers using numeral cards 0 to 9 and counters or coins.**

| 0 | 1 | 2 | 3 | 4 | 5 | 6 | 7 | 8 | 9 |

Spread out the cards face down. Choose two. Use the counters as decimal points. Make the largest and the smallest number you can. Write your result like this:

| 2 | • | 4 | < | 4 | • | 2 |

(**Remember**: You can use < to show 'less than' and > to show 'greater than'.)

Do this 10 times and write your results down

Now use three cards. Make as many two-digit decimals as you can. Put them in order.

For example, if you chose 4, 6 and 7, you would make 4.6, 6.4 and 4.7, 7.4 and 6.7, 7.6. In order they would be: 4.6, 4.7, 6.4, 6.7, 7.4, 7.6

you can use Workbook pages 55–59

Equivalent fractions

Use the fraction wall to help you compare fractions.
Fractions that are equal are called **equivalent fractions**.

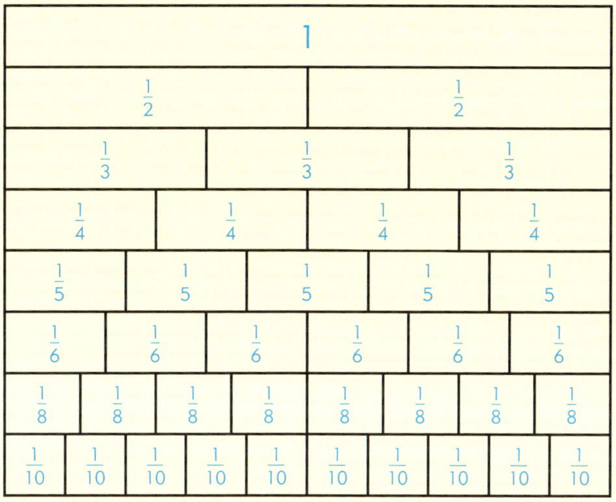

$\frac{1}{2} > \frac{1}{3}$ $\frac{2}{4} = \frac{1}{2}$ $\frac{1}{4} < \frac{1}{3}$

1 Name four fractions that are equivalent to $\frac{1}{2}$

2 Which fraction from the fraction wall is equivalent to:

a $\frac{2}{10}$? **b** $\frac{4}{10}$? **c** $\frac{6}{10}$? **d** $\frac{8}{10}$?

3 What pattern do you notice in your answers to question 2?

4 Fill in $<$, $>$ or $=$

a $\frac{1}{3}$ _____ $\frac{1}{4}$ **b** $\frac{3}{10}$ _____ $\frac{1}{5}$ **c** $\frac{3}{8}$ _____ $\frac{1}{2}$

d $\frac{3}{4}$ _____ $\frac{6}{8}$ **e** $\frac{4}{4}$ _____ $\frac{10}{10}$ **f** $\frac{3}{3}$ _____ $\frac{6}{6}$

5 Make up five of your own sentences showing equivalent fractions for the fraction wall.

you can use Workbook pages 60–4

Metric units of length

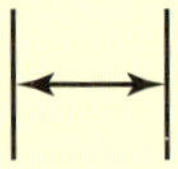

1 cm = 1 centimetre (cm)
100 cm = 1 metre (1 m)
1000 m = 1 kilometre (1 km)

1 **Use a ruler. Draw:**

- **a** a flower 4 cm high
- **b** a leaf 5.5 cm high
- **c** a stick 7 cm long.

2 **Say whether you would measure the following objects in metres, centimetres or kilometres:**

- **a** the length of your little finger
- **b** the length of your classroom
- **c** the distance from your home to school
- **d** the height of a wall
- **e** the length of a pen.

3 **Write these measurements in centimetres (cm):**

a 2 m **b** 3.5 m **c** 6.7 m

4 **Write these measurements in metres (m):**

a 150 cm **b** 785 cm **c** 1923 cm
d 2 km **e** 7.8 km **f** 3.4 km

you can use Workbook page 65

The delivery van

The van driver has to deliver to all these villages.

This map has a scale of 1 cm : 1 km

The van driver starts from Frio every day.

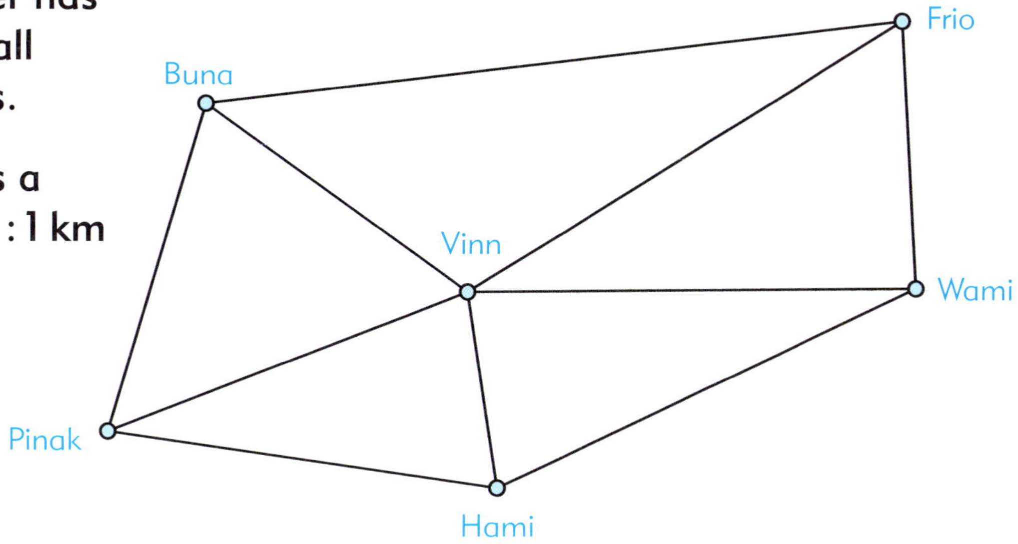

1 Use a ruler to measure the distance on the map and answer these questions.

a On Monday he has deliveries at Wami, Vinn and Pinak. How long is his shortest route in kilometres?

b What is his shortest route back to Frio? How long is it?

c On Tuesday he has to visit Buna and Hami. How long is his shortest route?

d On his return journey he has to make last-minute stops at Wami and Vinn. Which order should he visit them in to make the shortest trip?

e How long is the shortest route to visit every village and return to Frio? List the villages in order of deliveries.

2 Measure the items below. Choose what to measure with and whether to use km, m or cm.

a The perimeter of a door.

b The perimeter of the classroom.

c The perimeter of the playground.

you can use Workbook page 66

A maze in millimetres

Here is a maze. It is drawn using millimetres.

Remember: There are 10 mm in 1 cm.

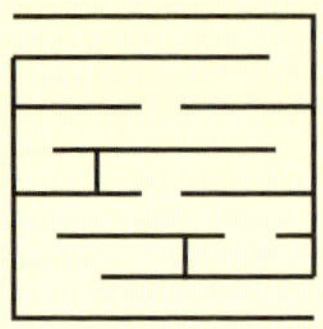

1 **Draw the maze again, but for every millimetre use 1 cm.**

a In a group, use chalk and a metre ruler. Draw the maze again on the playground, but for every millimetre use 1 m.

b Draw your own mini-maze in millimetres. Enlarge it to centimetres and metres.

2 **These sentences are written without the units km, cm, mm. Write them again, but put in sensible units.**

a At 11 years old, Sarah was 142 ___ tall.

b After driving for 68 ___, Marcel reached the next town.

c When Asif had sharpened his pencil, the point was 5 ___ long.

d Anita needed another 10 ___ strip of card to finish her model.

e My fingernail is 9 ___ wide.

f Abdul has a new mobile phone that is 8 ___ thick.

g Nita has just finished a 10 ___ run.

h Khalid and Sara drive about 5 ___ to school.

you can use workbook pages 67–8

Decimal fractions in pictures

100 square

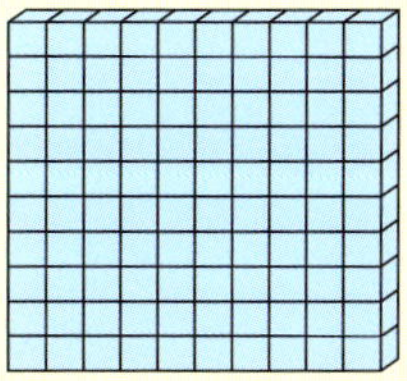

1 whole one
1.0

If 100 squares make 1 whole, then the 10 square strip is $\frac{1}{10}$ of the square.

We write these fractions as decimals like this: 0.1

10 long

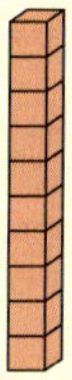

$\frac{1}{10}$
0.1

1 **Write the decimal and fraction that these show.**

a

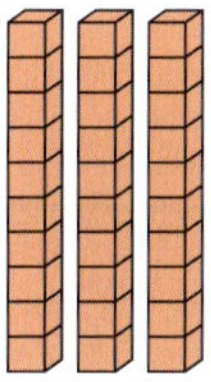

b

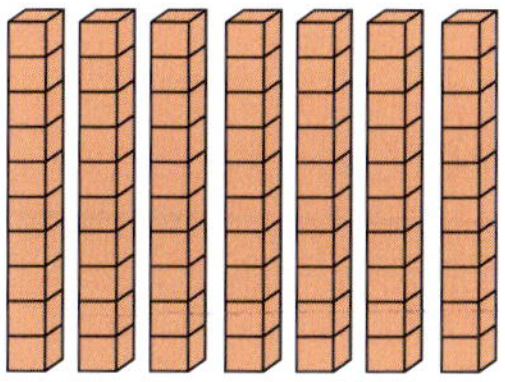

c

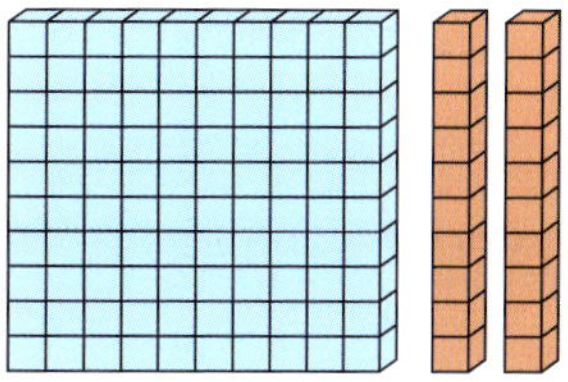

d

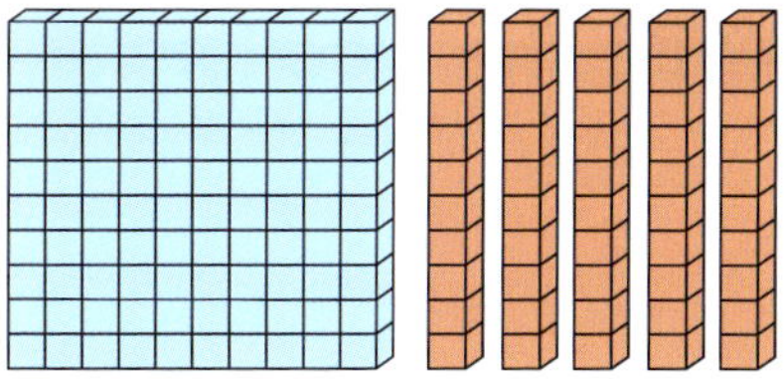

e

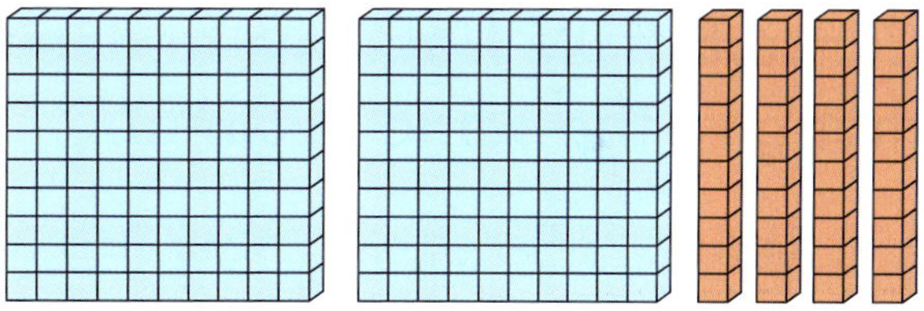

2 **Write the decimal and fraction that these abacus pictures show.**

a

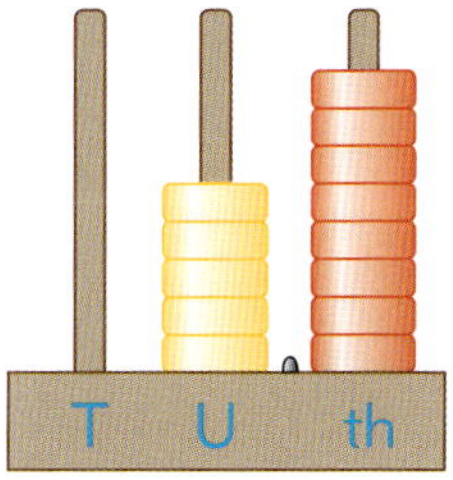

b

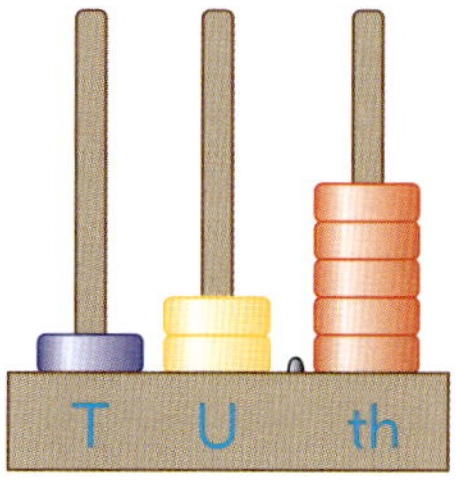

c

3 **Write the decimal and fraction shown by the coloured arrows on this number line.**

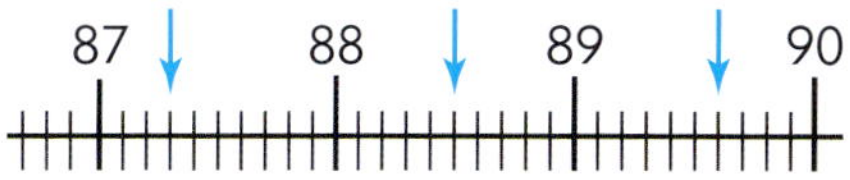

you can use Workbook page 69

Other fractions as decimals

To convert a fraction to a decimal, divide the top number (numerator) by the bottom number (denominator). Use a calculator.

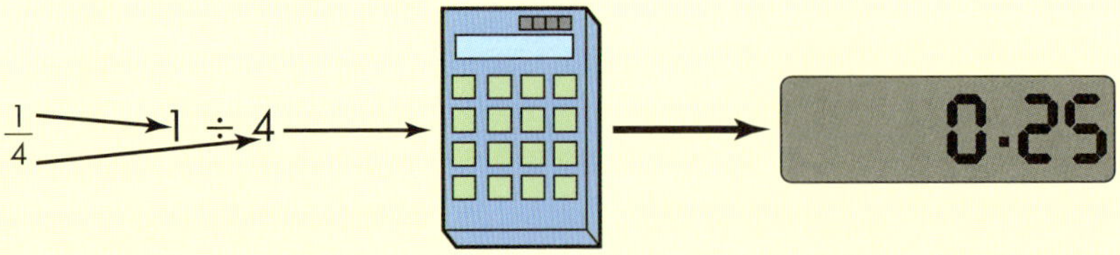

1 **Convert these fractions to decimals with the calculator.**

a $\frac{1}{2}$	**b** $\frac{3}{4}$	**c** $\frac{1}{3}$	**d** $\frac{2}{3}$
e $\frac{1}{5}$	**f** $\frac{2}{5}$	**g** $\frac{3}{5}$	**h** $\frac{4}{5}$
i $\frac{1}{6}$	**j** $\frac{2}{6}$	**k** $\frac{3}{6}$	**l** $\frac{5}{4}$

2 **Convert these fractions to decimals. Write the fractions in pairs that give the same decimal.**

$\frac{4}{6}$ $\frac{5}{10}$ $\frac{4}{8}$ $\frac{6}{8}$ $\frac{2}{3}$ $\frac{3}{4}$ $\frac{2}{6}$ $\frac{1}{3}$

3 **Choose a 'family' of fractions like sevenths ($\frac{1}{7}$).**

Use a calculator to convert them to decimals.

Make a chart like this one.

fraction	decimal
$\frac{1}{7}$	0.1428571
$\frac{2}{7}$	0.2857142
$\frac{3}{7}$	0.4285714

Describe any patterns you see.

Good fractions to try are ninths and elevenths, but try others too.

Hundredths

These pictures show tenths and hundredths and how to write them as decimals.

three tenths

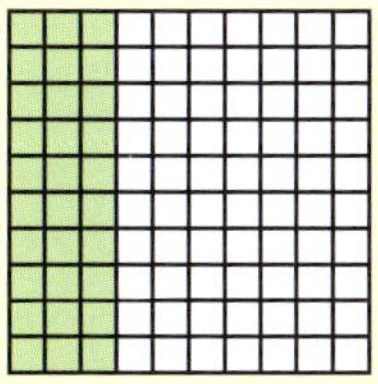

units	tenths
0	• 3

0.3

five hundredths

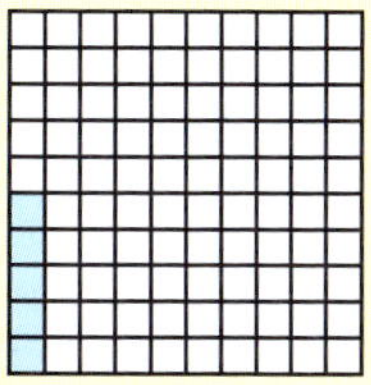

units	tenths	hundredths
0	• 0	5

0.05

thirty-five hundredths

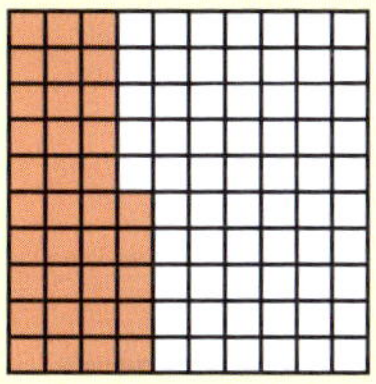

units	tenths	hundredths
0	• 3	5

0.35

1 Write the decimals shown by these pictures. Draw a chart if it helps.

a

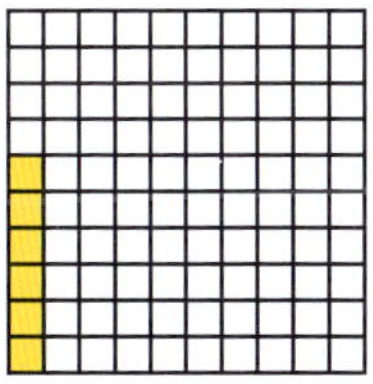

b

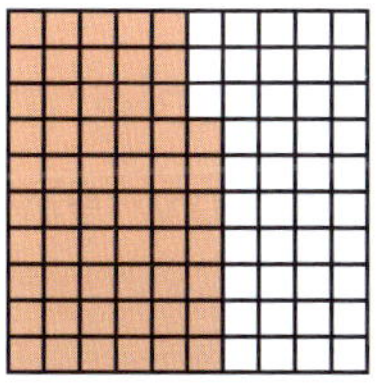

c

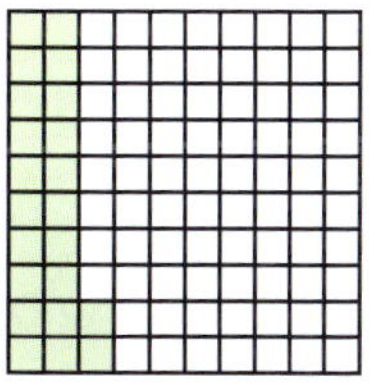

d

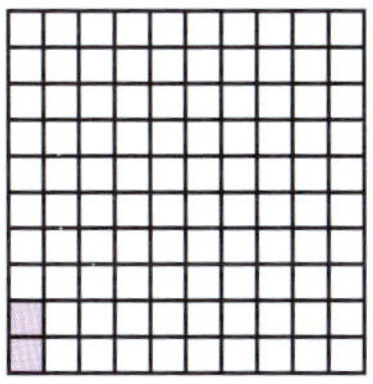

e

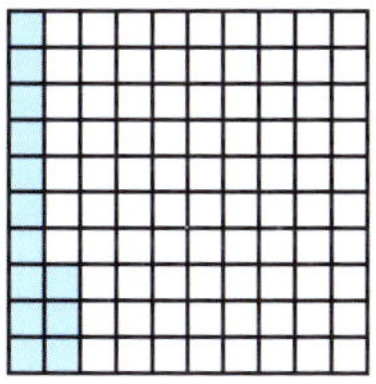

d

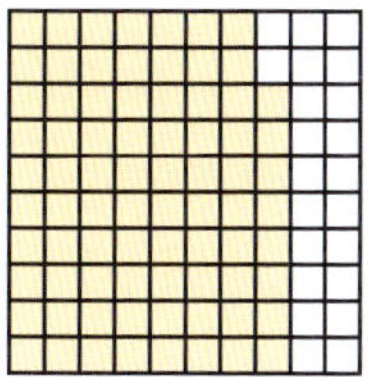

2 Use squares marked in hundreds. Colour these amounts.

a

units	tenths	hundredths
0	• 0	7

b

units	tenths	hundredths
0	• 4	5

c

units	tenths	hundredths
0	• 1	8

Decimal money

100c = $1   150c = $1.50   105c = $1.05

1 Write these amounts in dollars ($).

a 175c   **b** 225c   **c** 309c

d 580c   **e** 1260c   **f** 2505c

g 1995c   **h** 4999c   **i** 7004c

2 Write these amounts in cents (c).

a $0.50   **b** $0.05   **c** $5.55

d $4.70   **e** $15.25   **f** $29.99

3 Amina measured her height. She wrote it in two ways:

Name	cm	m
Amina	136	1.36

Measure your height and the heights of four friends. Make a chart. Show your heights in two ways.

4 Write a square marked in hundredths. Create designs by colouring in. Colour 0.24 of the square in one colour and 0.76 in another.

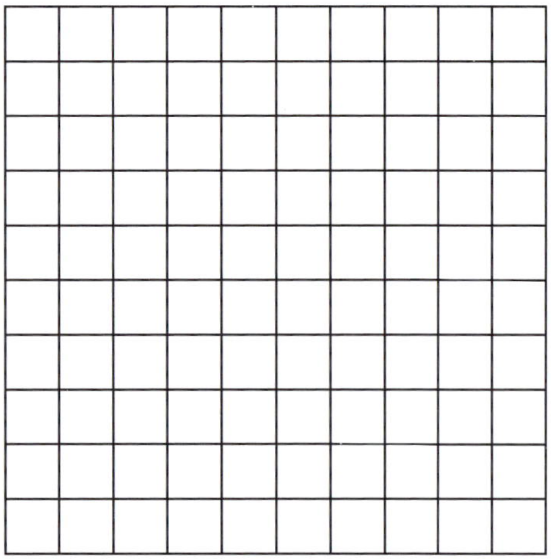

Comparing decimals

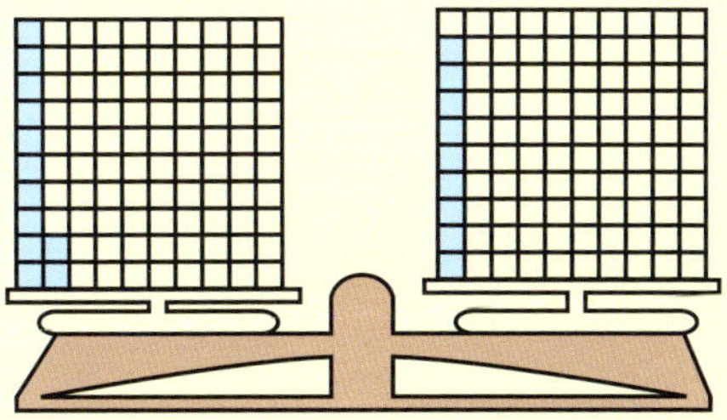

0.12 > 0.09

0.12 is greater than 0.09
0.12 > 0.09

0.22 < 0.28

If the tenths are the same, look at the hundredths.
0.22 is less than 0.28
0.22 < 0.28

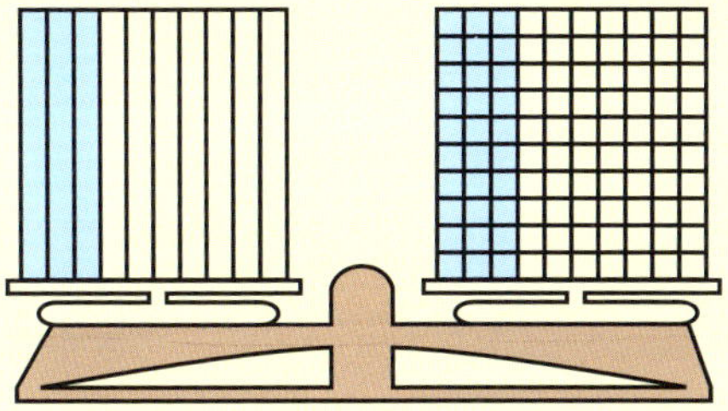

0.3 = 0.30

Sometimes numbers are equal.
0.3 = 0.30

1 **How much is shaded? Write the fractions. Then use >, <, or = to make true statements.**

a

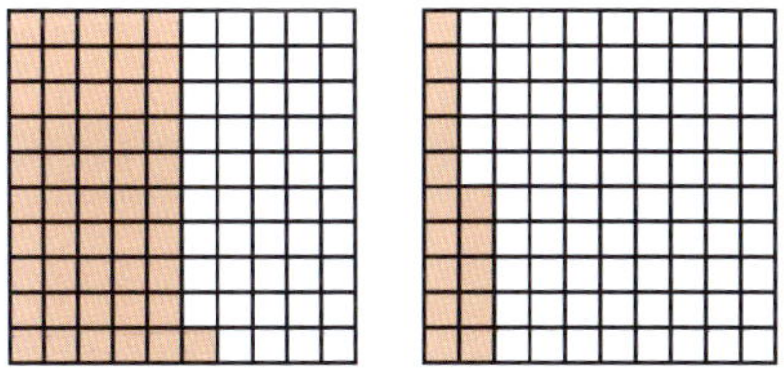

b

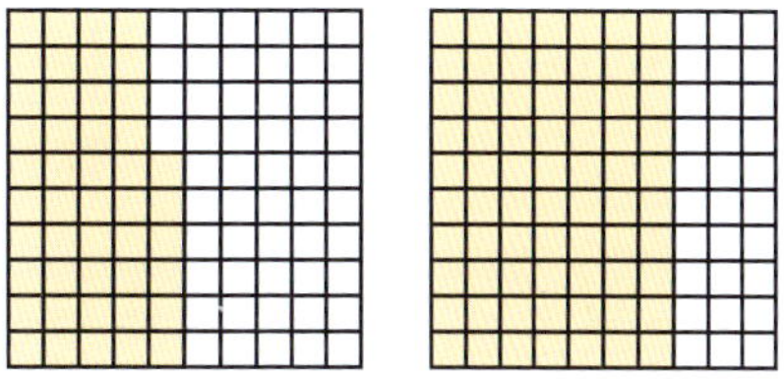

c

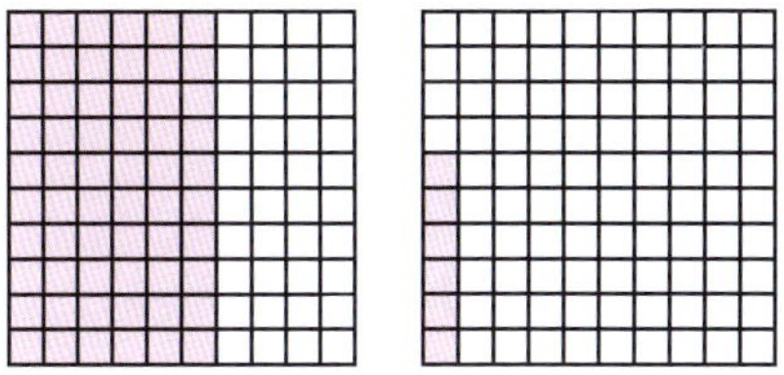

d

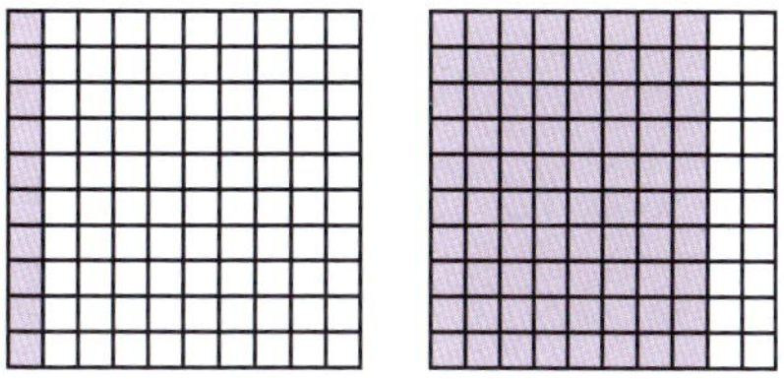

2 **Write >, < or = to make true statements.**

a 0.26 ___ 0.52 **b** 0.13 ___ 0.13 **c** 0.64 ___ 0.46 **d** 0.07 ___ 0.7

Putting decimals in order

1 **Write the next three numbers in these series.**

a 0.26, 0.27, 0.28, ___, ___, ___

b 1.96, 1.97, 1.98, ___, ___, ___

c 6.25, 6.24, 6.23, ___, ___, ___

d 8.04, 8.03, 8.02, ___, ___, ___

2 **Put these numbers in order from least to greatest.**

a 2.26, 1.85, 2.9, 1.35

b 1.04, 0.40, 1.01, 1.4

c 2.79, 5.12, 2.17, 1.38

d 1.25, 3.03, 2.71, 1.48

3 **Put these lists in order from greatest to least.**

a

Apple juice	\$1.39
Mineral water	\$0.69
Mayonnaise	\$1.09
Fromage frais	\$0.45
Orange and passionfruit	\$2.32
Satsuma juice	\$1.38
Apricot halves	\$0.52
Blackberries	\$1.50
Half-fat milk	\$0.30
Granary loaf	\$0.65

b

Bathroom accessories:	
Gold-plated mirror	\$22.99
Tumbler and holder	\$9.50
Soap dish	\$10.99
Shelf	\$14.99
Towel rail	\$14.95
Towel ring	\$9.95
Toilet-roll holder	\$9.99
Toilet-brush holder	\$24.99

4 **It helps to work out a bill quickly if you 'round' the amounts.**

If the amounts on a bill are \$1.99 and \$1.45, \$1.99 rounds up to \$2.00 and \$1.45 rounds down to \$1.00. The approximate cost is \$3.00 (the exact total is \$3.44).

a Use the food bill in question 3a above. Round all the prices up or down. What is the approximate total cost?

b Now use a calculator to add up the real bill. How close are the two answers?

Assessment 3

1 **Look at this pattern. Describe how it grows.**

Write the next two numbers and draw the next two shapes.

2 **A librarian collected the following data about the books in one section of the library.**

Picture books	II
Crime	𝍸 𝍸 𝍸 𝍸 𝍸 𝍸 𝍸 IIII
Romance	𝍸 𝍸 𝍸 𝍸 𝍸 𝍸 𝍸 III
Mystery	𝍸 𝍸 𝍸 𝍸 𝍸 𝍸 𝍸 𝍸 𝍸
Non-fiction	𝍸 𝍸 𝍸 𝍸 III
Reference	𝍸 𝍸 𝍸 II

a Use the librarian's tally chart to draw a frequency diagram.

b Which kind of book is there most of in this section?

c Do you think it was a children's section or an adults' section? Give a reason for your answer.

d How many books did the librarian count altogether?

3 **Write what fraction is shown by the shaded area of each shape.**

a

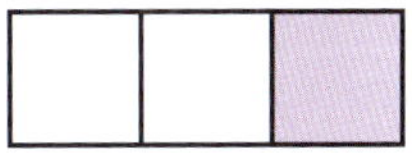

b

c

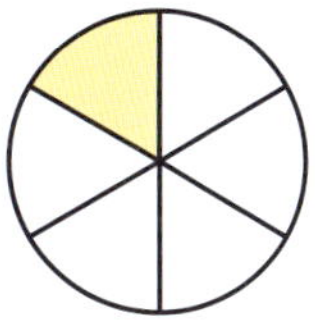

d

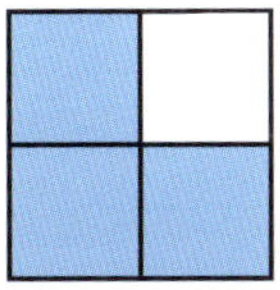

e

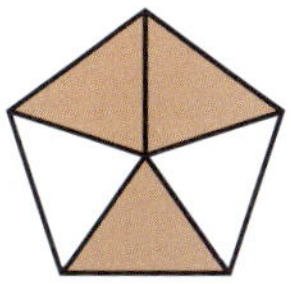

f

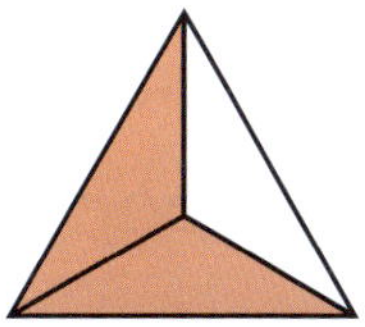

Assessment 3

4 **Draw your own shapes. Shade part of each shape to show these fractions:**

a $\frac{3}{4}$ **b** $\frac{5}{6}$ **c** $\frac{1}{2}$

5 **Solve these problems.**

a Joseph and his friends each ate $\frac{1}{2}$ a pizza.

They finished 5 pizzas altogether. How many friends were with Joseph?

(Hint: Remember to include Joseph in working out your answer!)

b A team of six runners shared some energy drinks. Each person drank $1\frac{1}{4}$ bottles. How many bottles did they finish altogether?

c If 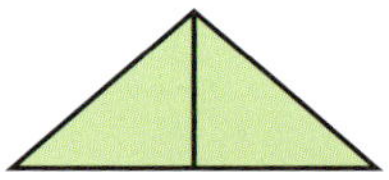 is 1,

then 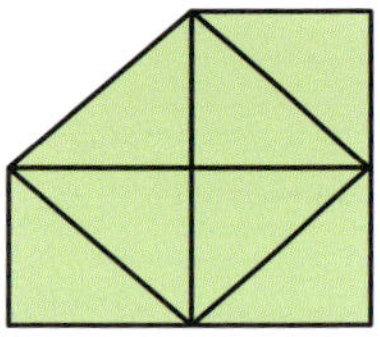 equals?

d If 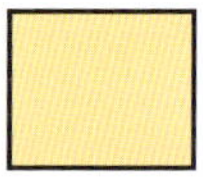 is 1,

then 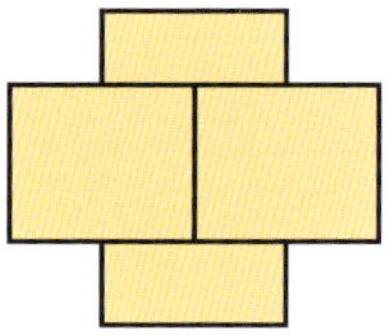 equals?

6 **a** Draw a picture or pattern using six horizontal lines and three vertical lines.

b Draw a pattern using only horizontal lines.

c Draw a pattern using only vertical lines.

7 **Write directions using the words 'horizontal', 'vertical', 'up', 'down', 'left' and 'right'.**

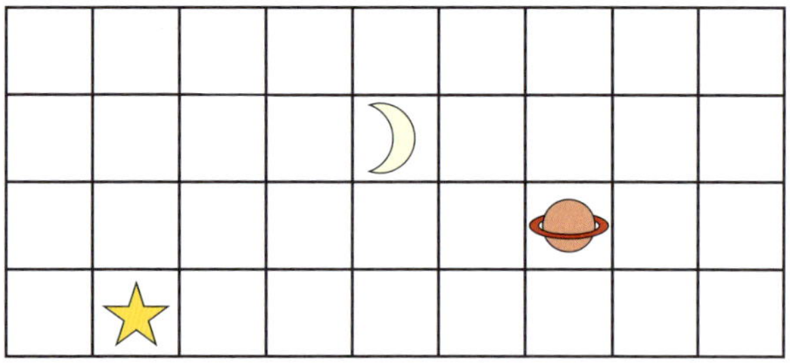

a to get from the moon to the star

b to get from the star to the planet

c to get from the moon to the planet.

Assessment 3

8 Write each of the following fractions as decimals.

a $\frac{1}{2}$ **b** $\frac{3}{10}$ **c** $4\frac{7}{10}$

9 Write two different equivalent fractions for each of the following.

a $\frac{3}{4}$ **b** $\frac{3}{5}$ **c** $\frac{7}{10}$

10 Write each of the following as fractions.

a 0.4 **b** 1.82 **c** 13.2

d 17.23 **e** 2.6 **f** 2.06

11 Write the following sets of decimals in order from smallest to greatest.

a 2.1, 1.2, 1.02, 2.11, 1.22, 2.02

b 7.8, 7.2, 7.5, 5.8, 5.18, 7.25, 7.85

Gymnastics

There are four main events in this gymnastics competition.

Here are the scores of five competitors.

	Vault	Bars	Floor	Beam
Francesca	8.50	7.65	8.00	7.15
Barbara	7.85	8.35	8.25	7.40
Mino	8.25	7.80	8.50	8.20
Denise	8.10	8.55	9.10	8.80
Olga	7.95	8.25	8.75	8.50

1 Use the information on the chart to help you answer these questions.

a What is the total score for each competitor? (Add their four scores to find out.)

b Write the total scores in order from greatest to least.

c Write the names of the winners of the gold, silver and bronze medals.

Decimals on your calculator

1 Add or subtract to get the number in the display. Use only the keys shaded green. You may use the keys more than once.

Write a number sentence for each one.

a

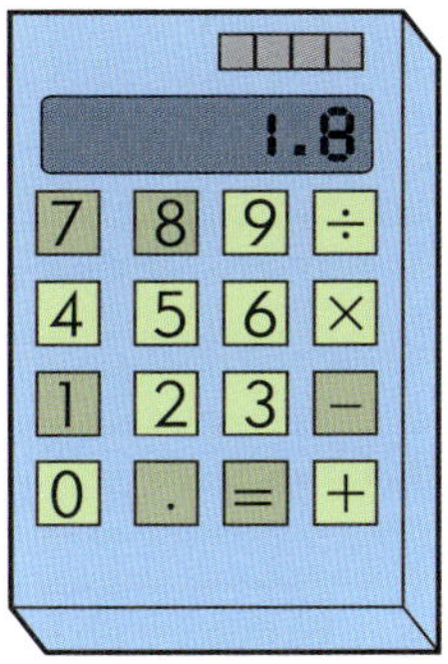

b

c

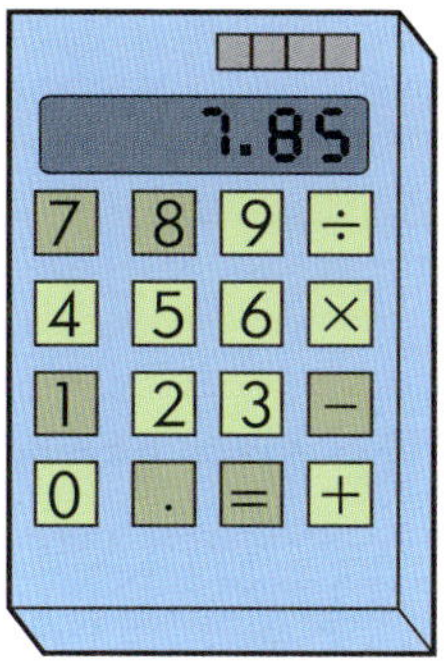

d

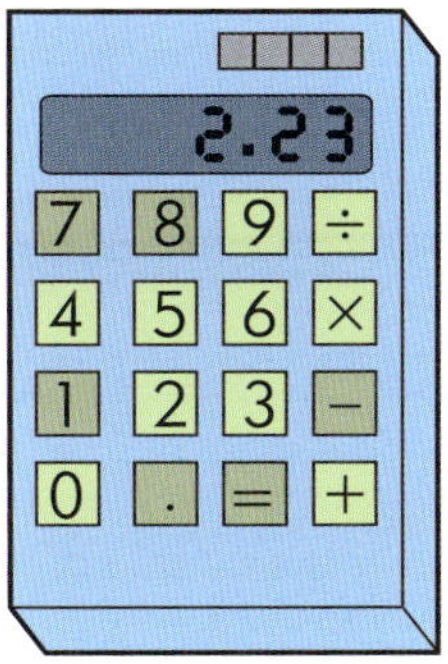

e

f

g

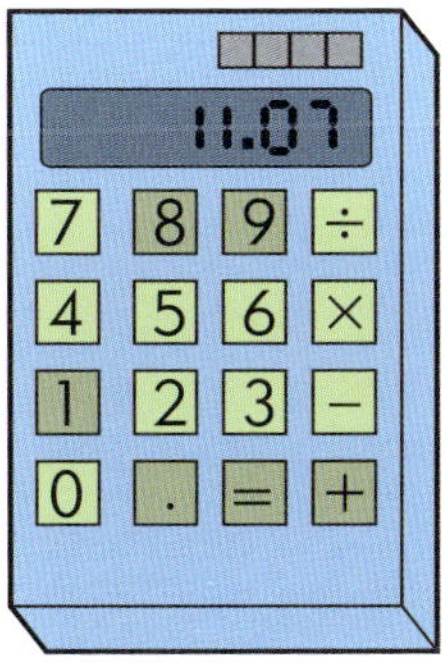

h

i

2 **What was the question?**

John ended up with 13.25 in his calculator display.

Write down two additions and two subtractions he might have used to get this answer.

Change the display

Chi Wing started with this number in his calculator: 42.73

He wanted to change it to 15.5

He wrote down the steps he took.

42.73 —(−20)→ 22.73 —(−7)→ 15.73 —(−0.03)→ 15.7 —(−0.2)→ 15.5

1 **Write the steps you take to change these numbers.**

a 25.34 → 5.2

b 16.25 → 50.75

c 48.3 → 10.55

d 16.5 → 8.25

e 29.75 → 58.25

f 17.35 → 34.7

You will need:

- a counter
- a calculator
- 2 sets of numeral cards 0 to 9

2 **Spread the cards out face down.**

Turn over 3 cards.

Use the counter to make a decimal number.

Put the number into your calculators.

Re-arrange the cards and counter to make a new number.

The winner is the person who changes the display to the new number in the fewest steps.

Percentages

Per cent means 'for each hundred'.

The symbol % means 'per cent'.

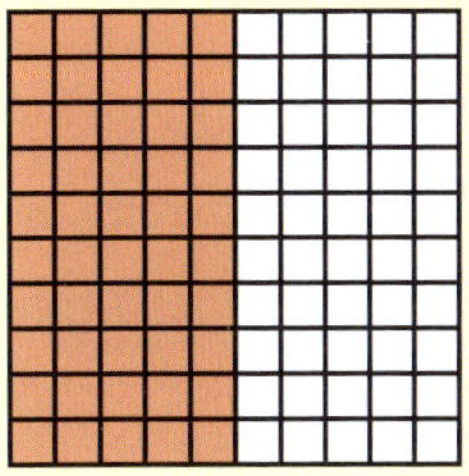

50% (or $\frac{1}{2}$) of this square is coloured red.

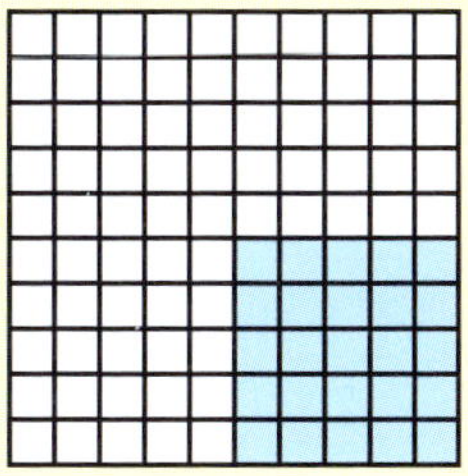

25% (or $\frac{1}{4}$) of this square is coloured blue.

1 **What percentage of these squares is shaded?**

a

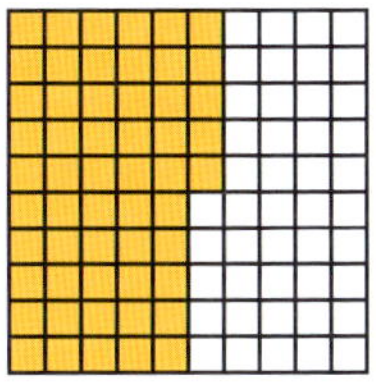

b

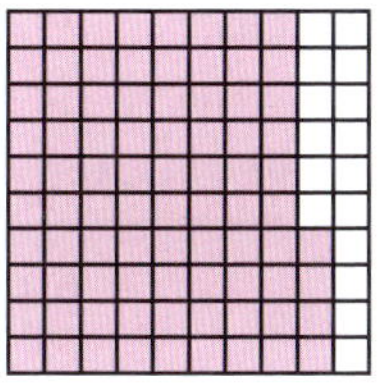

c

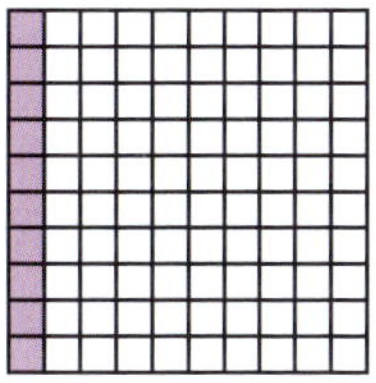

d

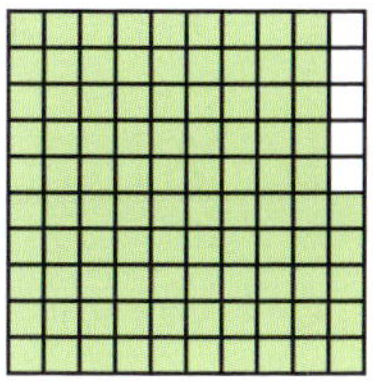

2 **Use 100 squares and colour these percentages.**

a 33% **b** 15% **c** 75%

3 **Richard answered 86 out of 100 questions correctly. What percentage did he score?**

4 **This sheet has 100 stickers.**

a What percentage of the stickers is stars?

b What percentage of the stickers is neither stars nor squares?

5 **Jenny has 100 stickers in her album; 63 of them are swaps that she made with her friends. What percentage of the stickers are not swaps?**

you can use Workbook page 70

More percentages

Remember: A percentage is a fraction out of 100.

$50\% = \frac{50}{100} = \frac{5}{10} = 0.5$

1 I finished half the questions in my homework.

a What percentage did I finish?

b What percentage are not yet finished?

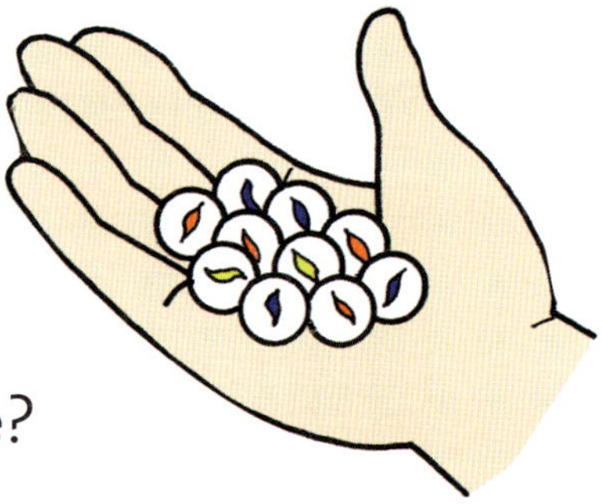

2 In a bag, 7 out of 28 marbles are blue.

a What fraction of the marbles are blue?

b What percentage of the marbles are blue?

c What percentage of the marbles are not blue?

3 20 people booked tickets for a show.

TICKET PRICES

Full price	\$10.00
Student price	\$7.00

Tuesdays: 2 tickets for \$10
NO STUDENT DISCOUNT
ON TUESDAYS!

5 paid the full price for tickets, 7 paid the student price, and the rest bought 2 for \$10.

a What percentage paid the full price?

b What percentage paid the student price?

c What percentage bought 2 for \$10?

d What was the total amount paid for all 20 seats?

Nets and boxes

When a box is flattened out to show its net, you can see its whole surface area.

Each of the 42 squares on this page represents 1 cm.

The surface area = 42 cm^2

Surface area 42 cm^2

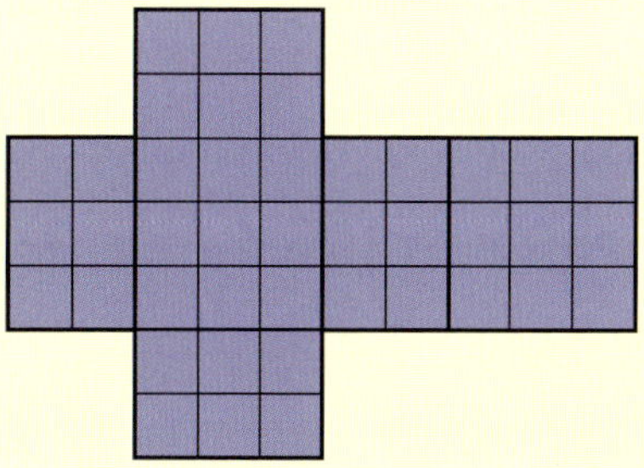

1 Find the surface areas of these nets.

a

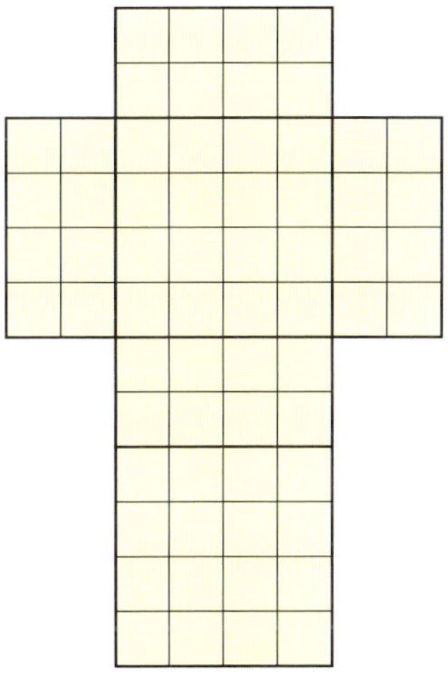

b

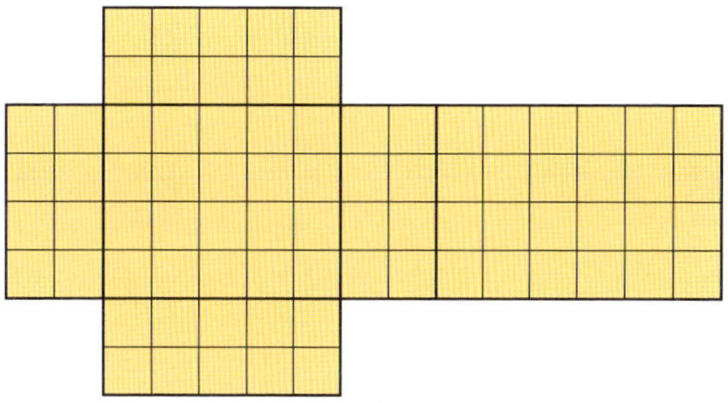

c

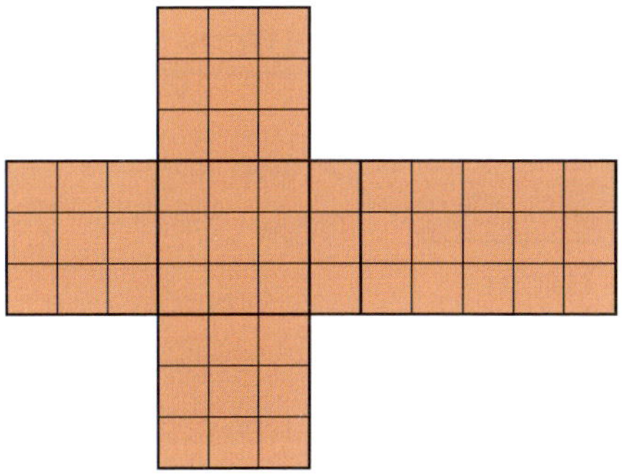

d

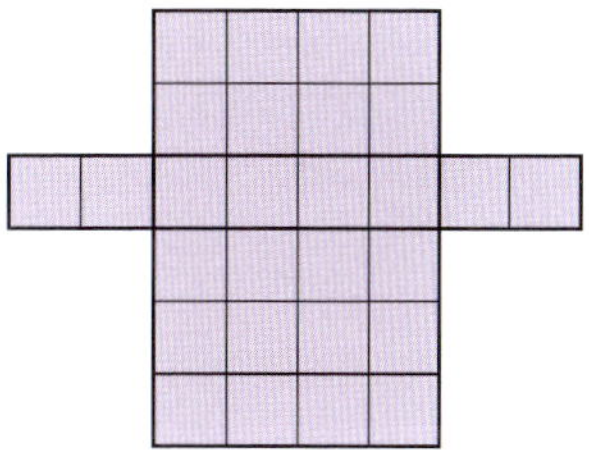

2 Use centimetre-squared paper to make a box from the net in question 1c above. How many centimetre cubes can you fit inside it?

Find the surface area

You can work out the surface area of a box by measuring length, breadth and height, and calculating the area of each face.

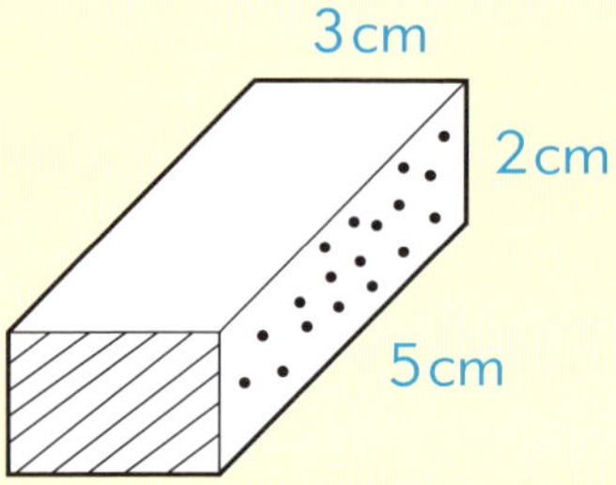

Remember: a box has 6 faces so you should have 6 areas to add up to find the total.

2 plain faces:	2 spotted faces:	2 striped faces:
5cm × 3cm = 15cm^2	5cm × 2cm = 10cm^2	3cm × 2cm = 6cm^2
5cm × 3cm = 15cm^2	5cm × 2cm = 10cm^2	3cm × 2cm = 6cm^2

Total 62cm^2

Find the surface areas of these boxes.

1

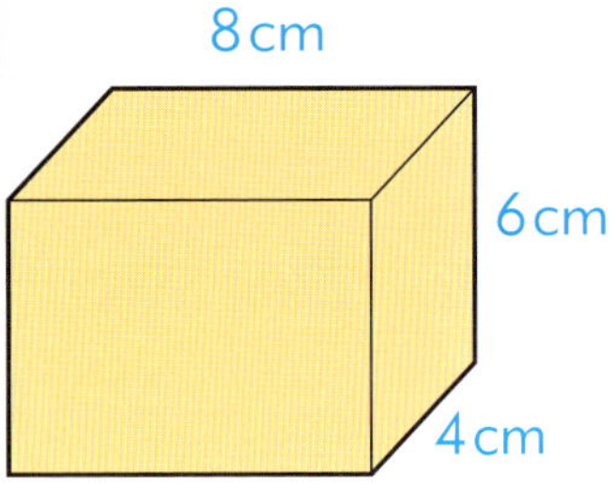

2

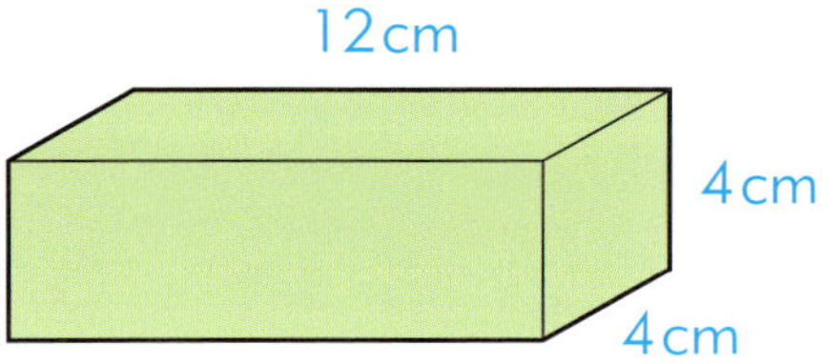

3

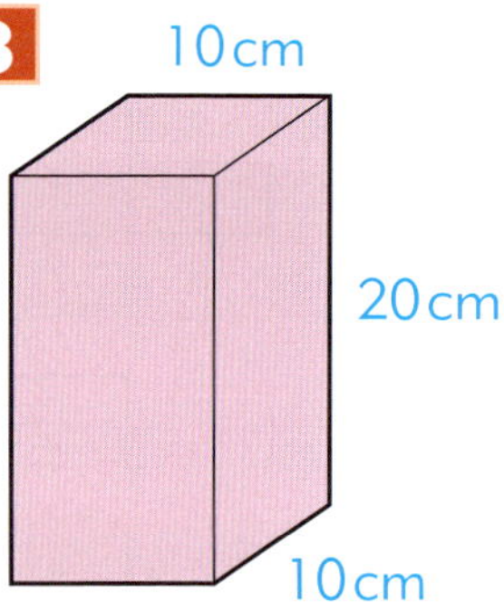

4

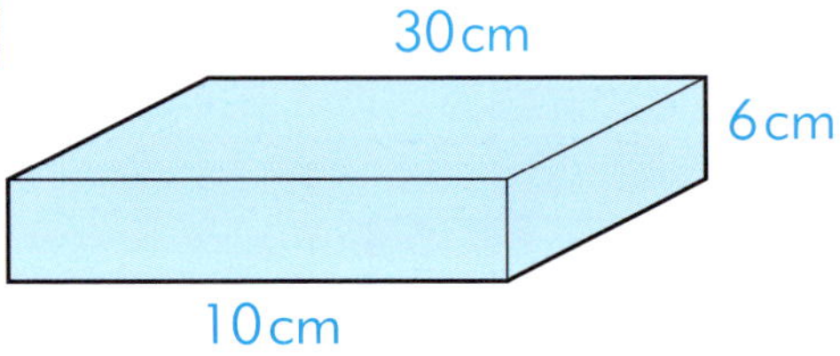

5

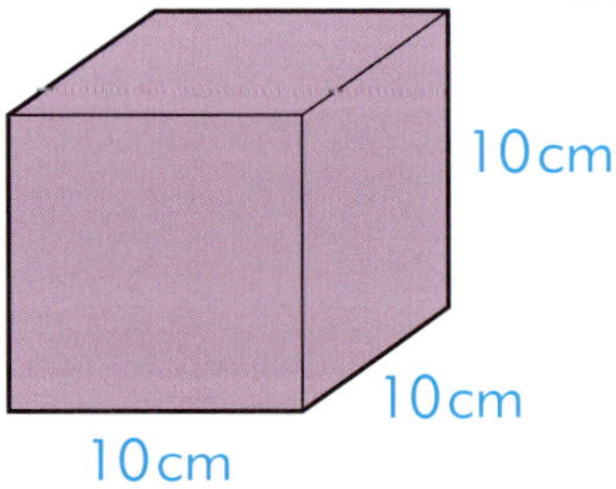

6

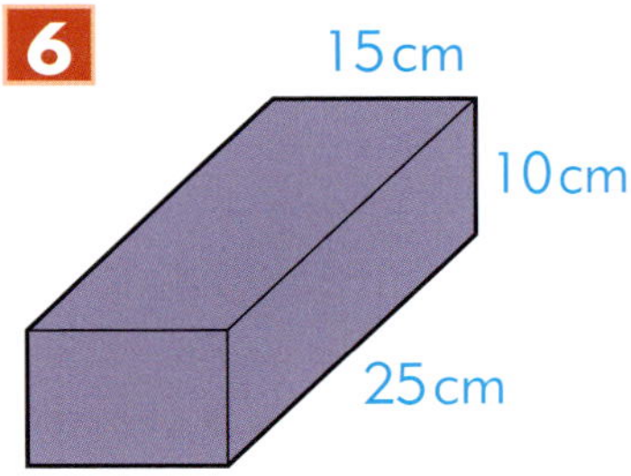

7

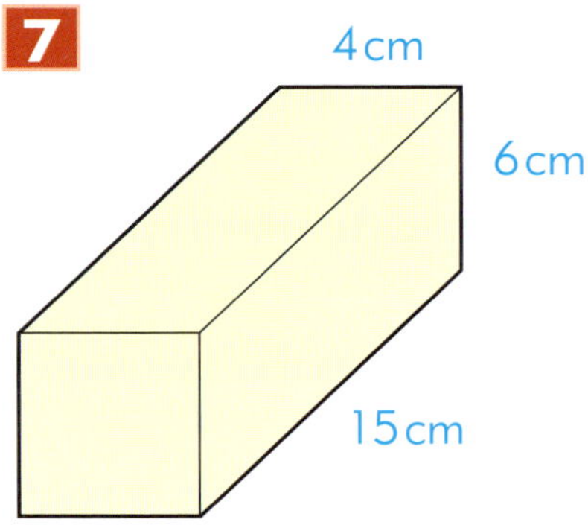

you can use Workbook pages 71–2

Complete the shape

Shapes can be made into rectangles by cutting and re-arranging.

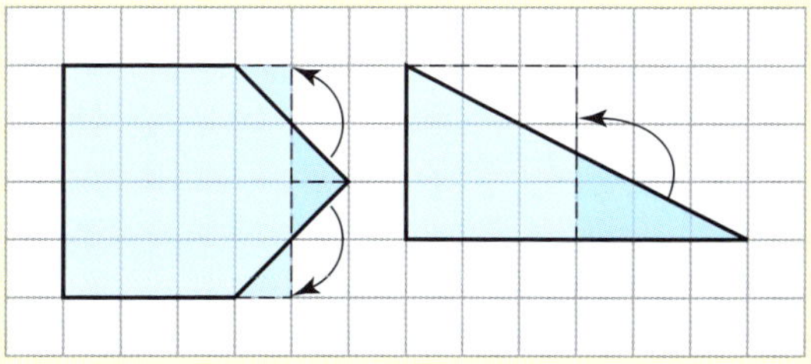

1 Draw these shapes on centimetre-squared paper. Cut and re-arrange them to make rectangles. Write the areas of the new rectangles.

a

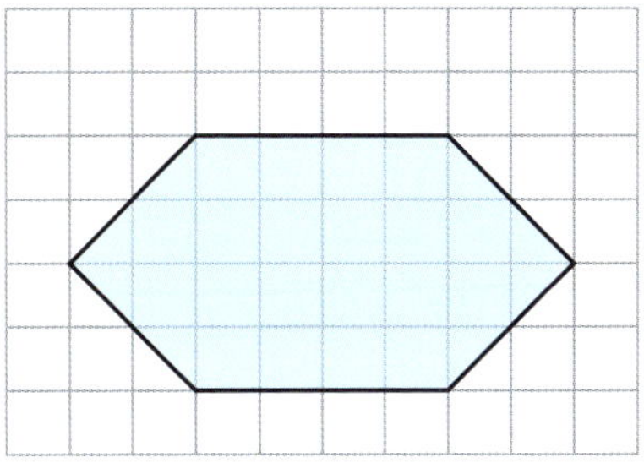

b

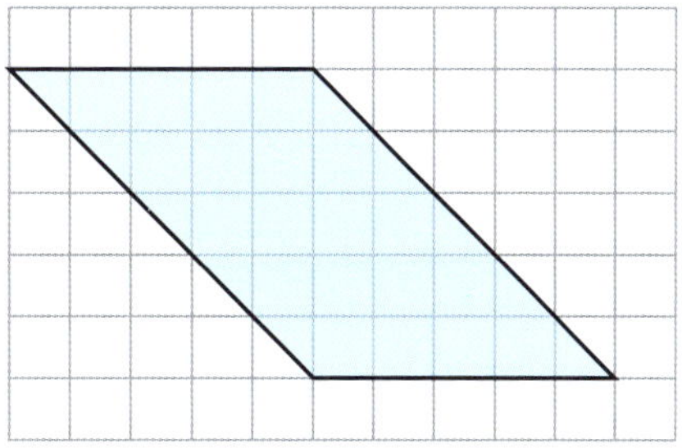

c

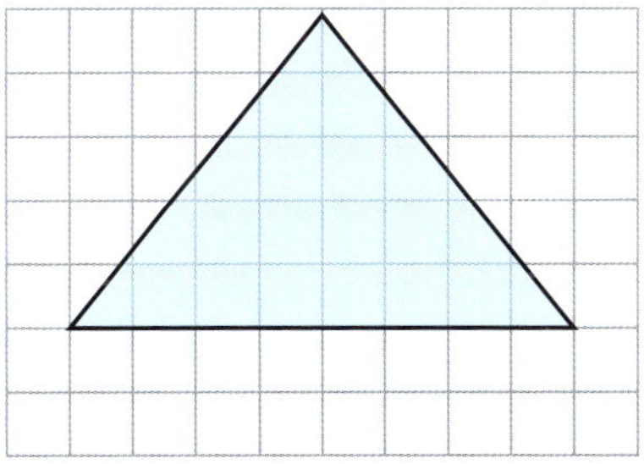

d

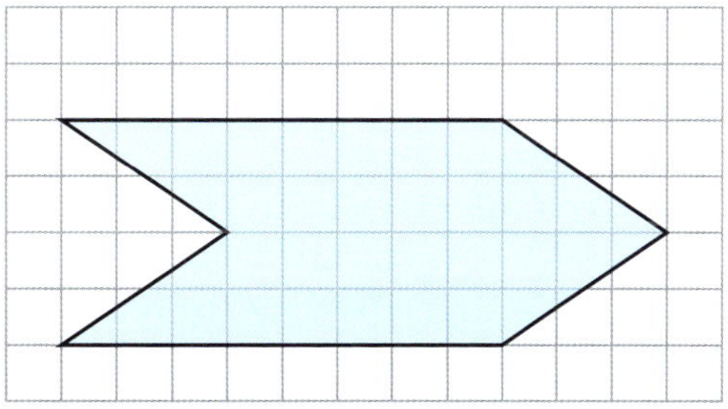

2 Draw some shapes of your own. Ask your friends to make them into rectangles. Find the areas together.

you can use workbook page 73

Areas of other shapes

This shaded area is 1 cm^2.

This shaded area is 0.5 cm^2.

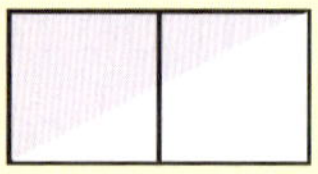

This shaded area is 1 cm^2.

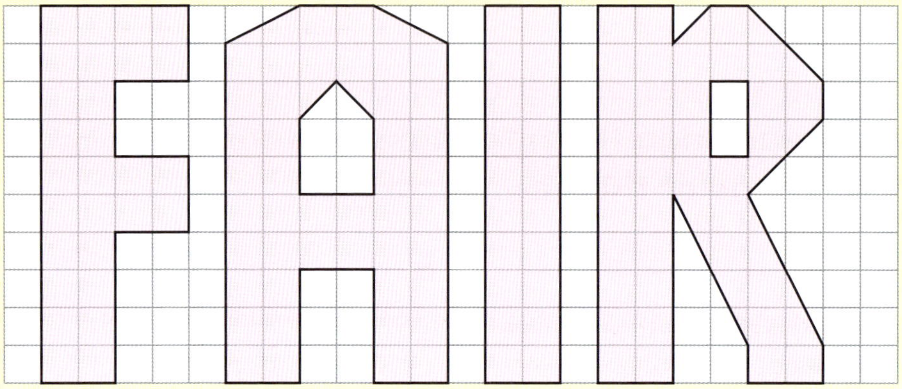

1 Using the word FAIR above, answer the following.

a Write the area of each letter.

b Write the total area covered by the whole word FAIR.

c Write the area of paper not covered by the word FAIR.

d Use centimetre-squared paper. Write your name or initials.

2 Use centimetre-squared paper to draw these shapes.

a An L covering 6 cm^2.

b A T covering 18 cm^2.

c A right-angled triangle covering 4.5 cm^2.

d an F covering 8 cm^2.

e An irregular hexagon covering 10 cm^2.

f A + sign covering 20 cm^2.

3 Try some shapes of your own and set them as puzzles for a friend.

you can use Workbook pages 74–6

How many rectangles?

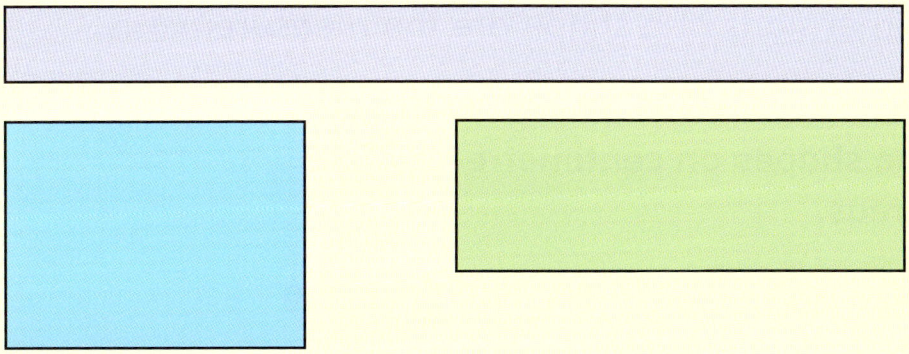

All of these rectangles have an area of 12 cm², but different lengths and breadths.

1 **Write down all the possible lengths and breadths of rectangles and squares with these areas. You may wish to draw them on squared paper.**

a 8 cm² **b** 16 cm² **c** 24 cm²
d 18 cm² **e** 36 cm² **f** 20 cm²

2 **In this series of shapes, one side increases in length by 1 cm each time. Make a chart like this one and continue the series. Describe any patterns you find.**

Length	Breadth	Area
1 cm	3 cm	3 cm²
2 cm	3 cm	6 cm²
3 cm	3 cm	9 cm²
4 cm	3 cm	12 cm²

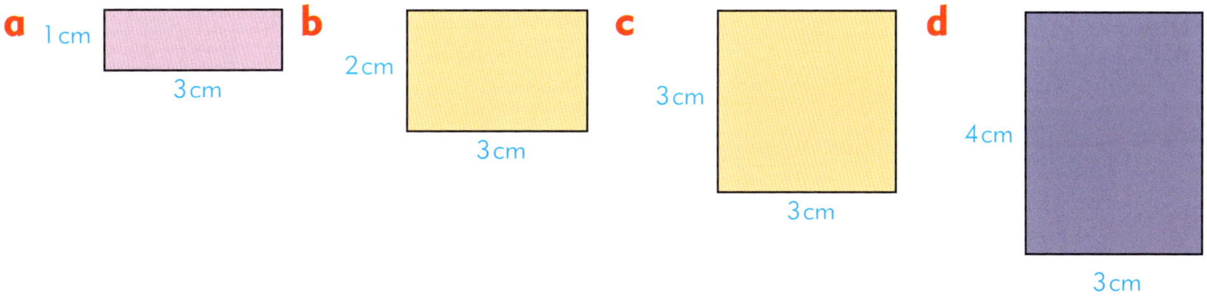

you can use Workbook page 77

Double the dimensions

Remember: The dimensions of a shape are the measurements.

Draw each of these shapes on centimetre-squared paper. Write the areas.

Double the dimensions of each shape and draw the larger shapes.

Write down the new areas. Write what you notice about the change in area.

1

2

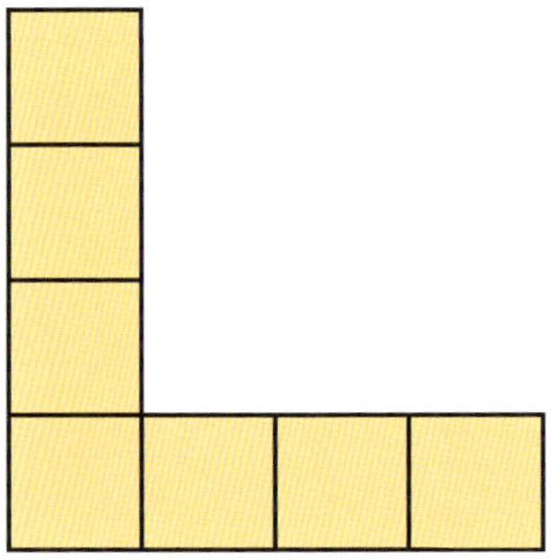

3

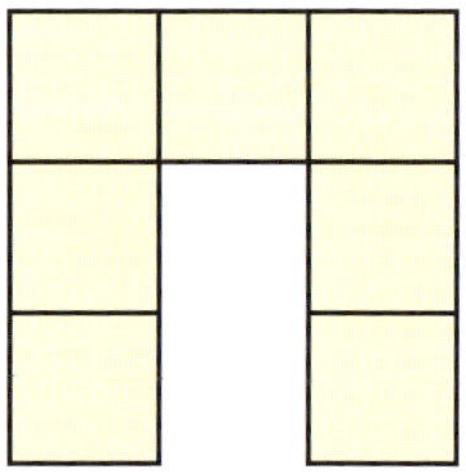

4

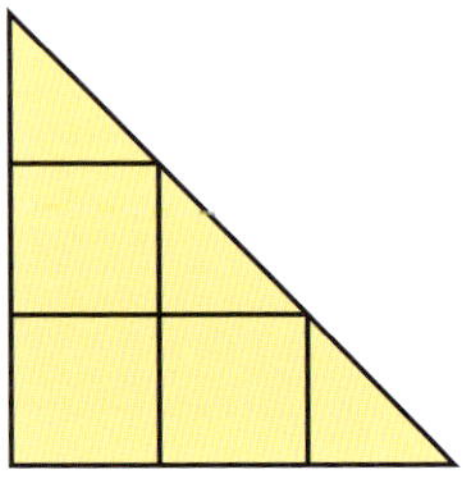

5

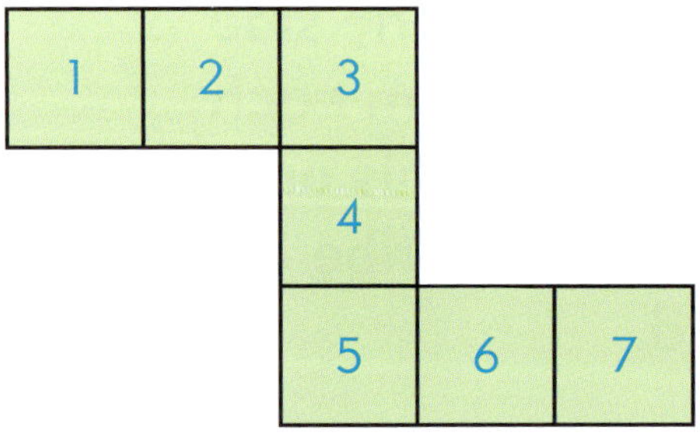

6

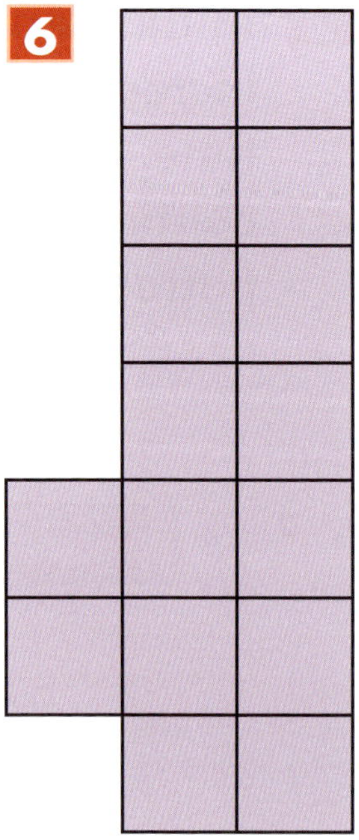

7

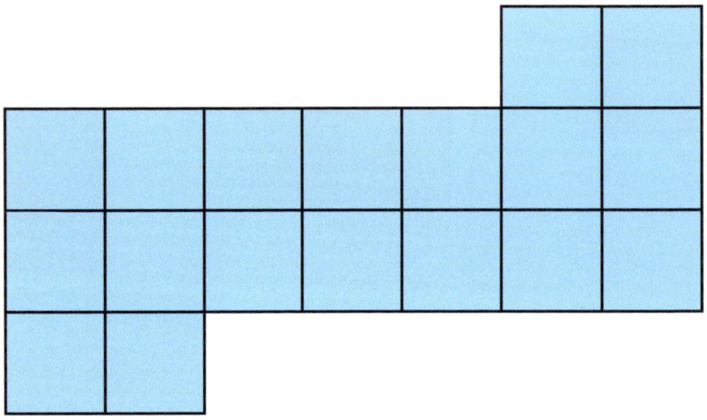

Naming triangles

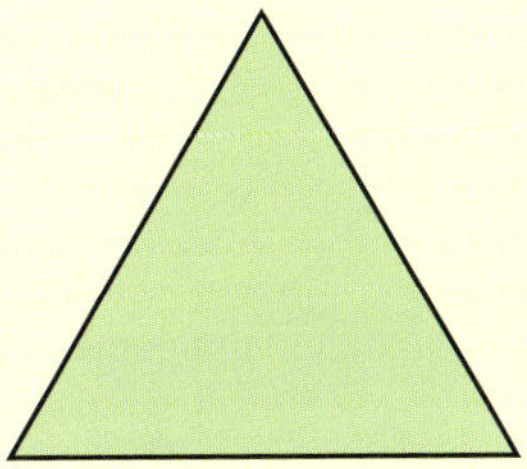

An equilateral triangle has all sides equal.

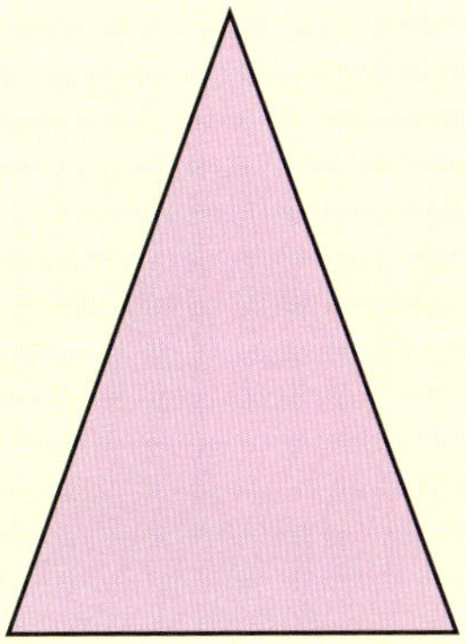

An isosceles triangle has two sides equal.

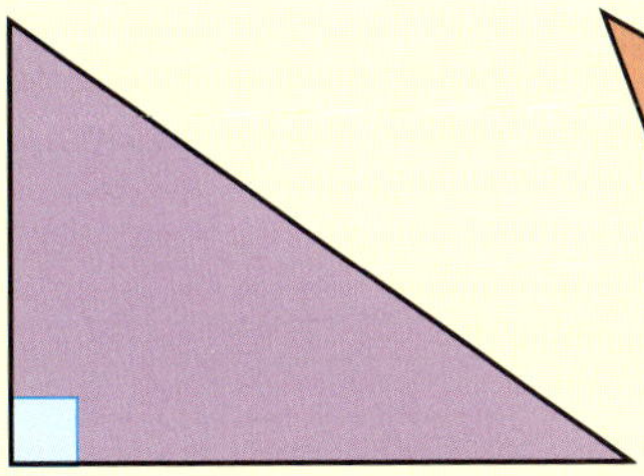

A right-angled triangle has one right angle.

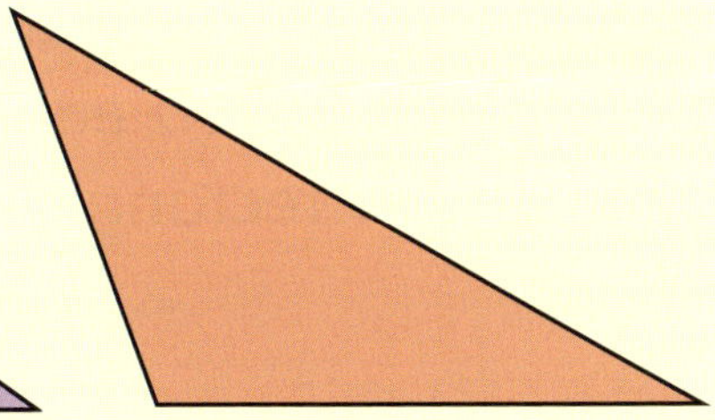

A scalene triangle has all sides of different lengths.

1 **Use a ruler and a right-angle measure or strip of card. Name these triangles.**

a

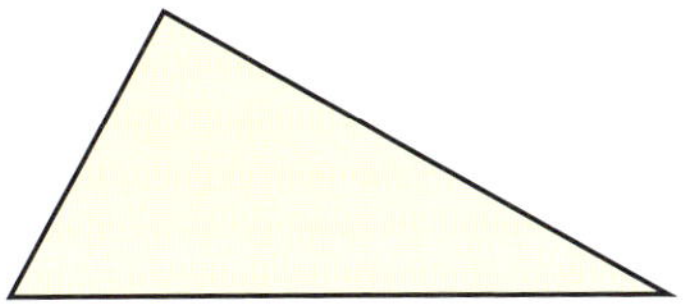

b

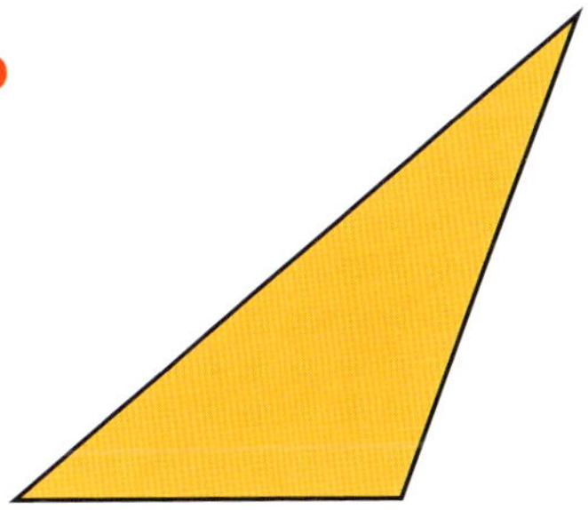

c

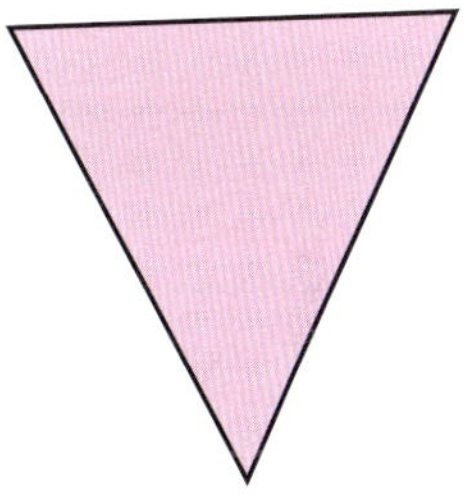

d

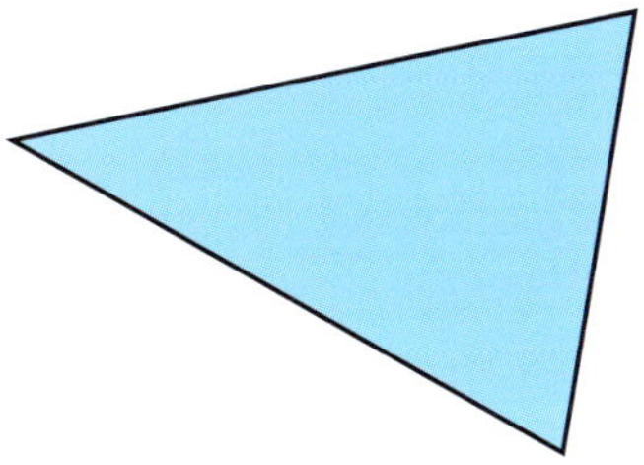

e

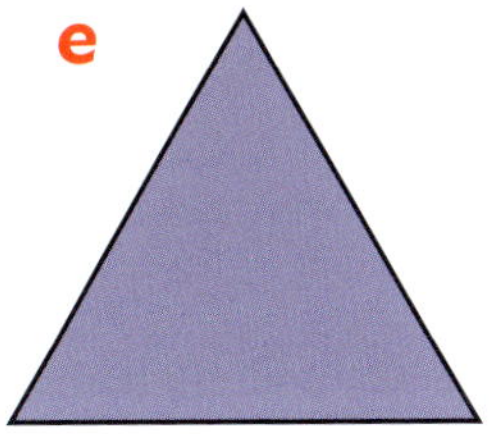

f

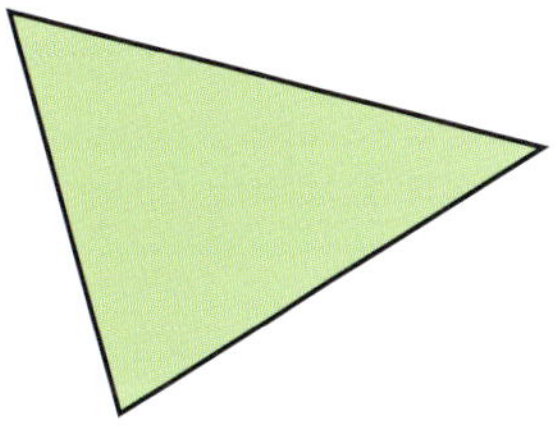

2 **Use either square or isometric paper.**

a Make each kind of triangle on your paper.

b Write the names of the ones that are easy to make.

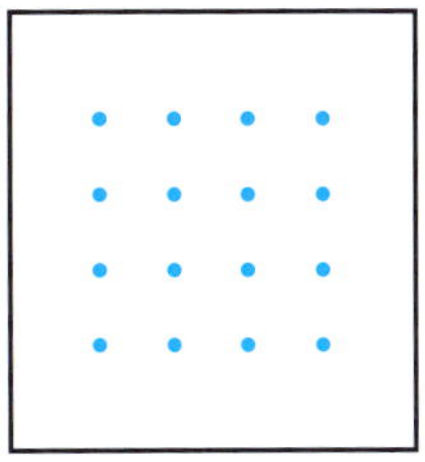

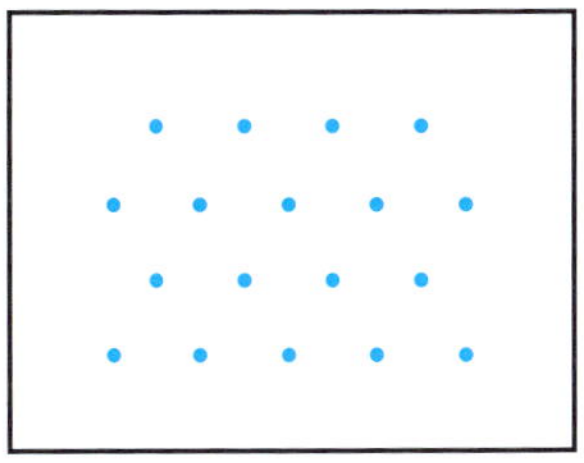

square or isometric

Squares, rectangles, rulers and set squares

A **set square** is a drawing instrument with a right angle.

You can use it with a ruler to make clear right-angled corners when you draw squares or rectangles.

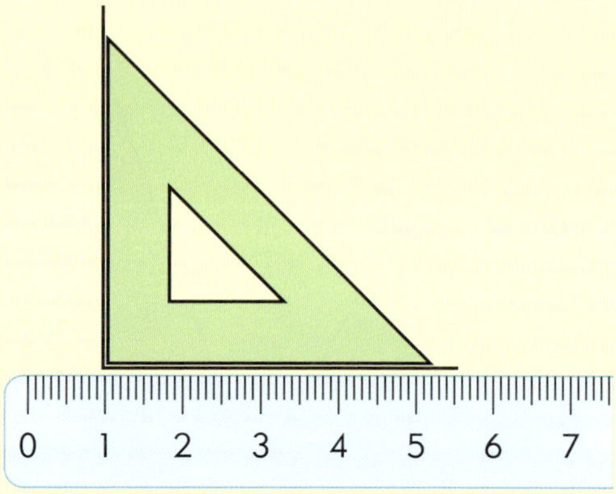

Use a ruler and set square to measure and copy these rectangles exactly on paper. Cut out your drawing and place them over the shapes to check how accurate they are.

1

2

3

4

5

6

Chains of numbers

Numbers can grow by repeating the same number operation many times.

Remember: You can set up a constant function on your calculator.

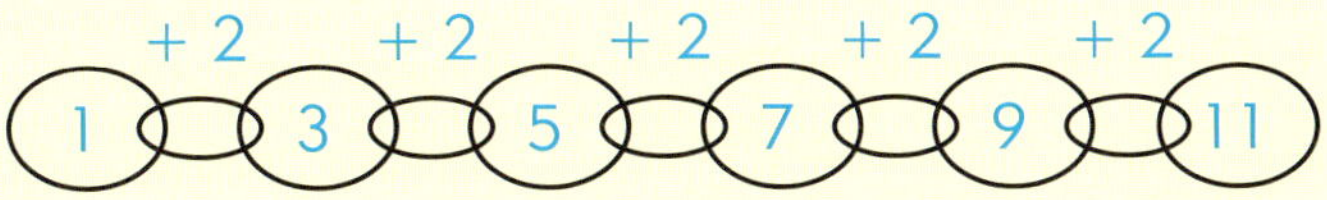

They can also get smaller. Notice there are two operations here.

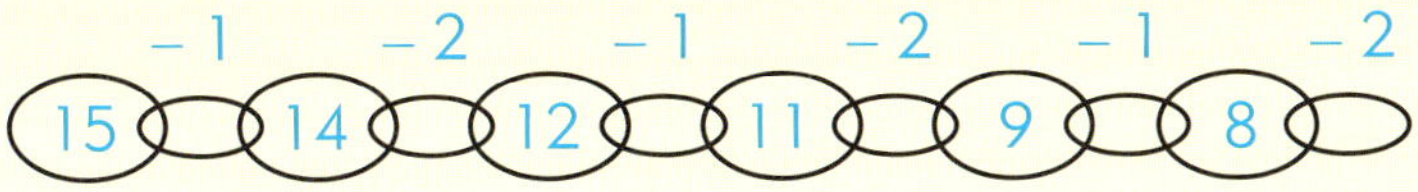

1 **Discover the hidden operations in these chains and continue them to their 10th number.**

a 4, 7, 10, 13, 16, …

b 42, 38, 34, 30, 26, …

c 3, 4, 8, 9, 18, 19, …

d 2, 4, 8, 16, 32, …

2 **Find the longest chain.**

Start with a two-digit number.	**84**
Multiply the two digits.	$8 \times 4 = 32$
Multiply the two digits in the result.	$3 \times 2 = 6$
This chain has three steps:	$84 \rightarrow 32 \rightarrow 6$

Try this with lots of two-digit numbers.

a What is the longest chain you can find?

b What is the shortest chain you can find?

c What end numbers can be made?

d What end numbers cannot be made?

Some more number chains

1 **Here are some more number chains to investigate.**

Start with any number 17

If it is odd ... add 1. 17 + 1 = 18

If it is even ... halve it. 18 ÷ 2 = 9

Carry on: 9 + 1 = 10 ÷ 2 = 5 + 1 = 6 ÷ 2 = 3 ⟶ ?

a Where does this chain end?

b Try lots of other starting numbers.
Where do their chains end?

2

Start with a two-digit multiple of 7.	**28**
Multiply the units digit by 5.	**8 × 5 = 40**
Add the tens digit to the result.	**40 + 2 = 42**
Multiply the units digit by 5 again.	**2 × 5 = 10**
Add the tens digit to the result.	**10 + 4 = 14**

a Continue this chain. Where does it end?

b Try other multiples of 7. What do you notice?

3

Start with any two-digit number.	**25**
Add the digits.	**2 + 5 = 7**
Square the result.	**7 × 7 = 49**

a Carry on with this chain. What happens?

b Try this with lots of different two-digit starting numbers.
What happens in each sequence?

Elephant house sums

The elephant's keeper puts different numbers of buns in each room of the elephant house.

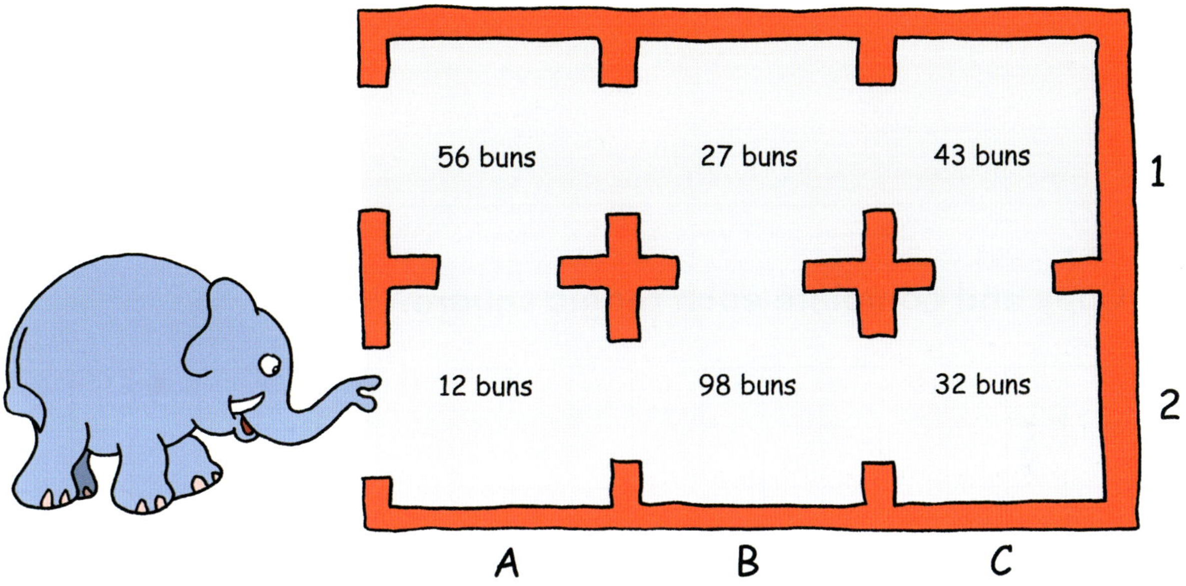

1 If the elephant went from A2 to A1 and then B1, how many buns could he eat?

2 How many would he eat for these routes?

a A1, B1, C1

b A2, B2, C2

c A1, B1, B2, C2

d A2, B2, B1, C1

3 If the elephant were allowed to eat buns in 3 rooms, which 3 rooms would give him the most buns? How many could he eat?

4 Draw your own elephant house with 8 rooms.

Put in some numbers. Make up some problems.

Magic squares

In a magic square, each row, column and diagonal has the same sum.

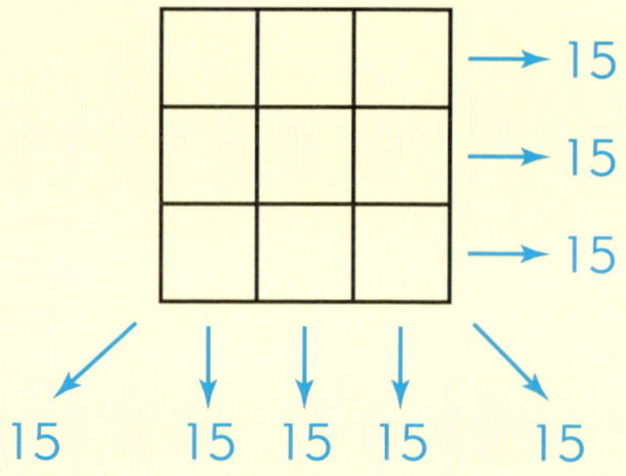

1 **Copy and complete each magic square.**

a

	2	
14	10	
4	18	8

b

	30	
	50	
	70	20

c

39		
43	38	
		37

d

12	27	6
24	3	

e

		100
	125	225
		50

2 **Choose any magic square from question 1. Multiply each number by 2. Do you still have a magic square?**

3 **Investigate subtraction and addition.**

Work through this example:

Write down a three-digit number.	**734**
Reverse it.	**437**
Take away.	**734 – 437 = 297**
Reverse it.	**792**
Add.	**297 + 792 = 1089**

a Try a different three-digit number and do the same. What do you notice?

b Try it with two-digit numbers. What do you notice about the answers?

c Try it with four-digit numbers. What do you notice?

Working with x and y

$x = 3, y = 7$

Solve: $x \times y$ $\qquad x \times y = 3 \times 7$

$\qquad\qquad\qquad\qquad = 21$

Sometimes we use letters to represent numbers. This is called **substitution**. We can use substitution to help solve problems.

1 **Solve these problems for $x = 3$, $y = 7$.**

a $y - x$ **b** $x + y$

2 **Solve these problems for $x = 15$, $y = 2$.**

a Multiply x and y.

b Find the difference between x and y.

c What is the total if you double x, double y and add them together?

3 **I have four times as many apples as pears. I have three bags of pears, each with 5 pears. Let x = the total number of apples and y = the total number of pears. Find x and y.**

4 **y is half of 90 and x is three times y. Find x and y.**

5 **$y = x + 5$ $\qquad x = 10 \times 7$ $\qquad$ Find x and y.**

6 **Solve for $x = 30$, $y = 40$.**

a Find the sum of half of x added to half of y.

b Find the difference between x and y.

Litres and millilitres

The **capacity** of a container tells us how much it can hold. The standard unit of capacity is the litre.

1 litre (1 l) = 1000 millilitres (1000 ml)

Measuring spoons and cups have exact capacities.

1 teaspoon	1 cup	500 ml	1000 ml
5 ml	250 ml	$\frac{1}{2}$ l	1 l

1 **Collect some containers from yoghurt, juice, milk and other liquids.**

a Arrange your containers in order from the one with the smallest capacity to the one with the biggest capacity. Try to estimate the capacity of each container.

b Use measuring jugs and spoons to measure the exact capacity of each container.

2 **You can check the answers to these questions using real measuring spoons and cups.**

a How many teaspoons in 1 cup?

b How many cups in 1 litre?

c How many cups in 2.5 litres?

3 **How many litres do you need to fill:**

a 8 cups **b** 9 cups **c** 11 cups **d** 22 cups

Lotions and potions

Remember: There are 1000 millilitres in a litre.

The short way of writing millilitres is ml

The short way of writing litres is l

1 **The professor makes his own lotions and potions. Here are some of his recipes for lotions. Write down how much liquid each one makes.**

a *Hair restorer lotion:*
250 ml beetroot juice
175 ml bath water
50 ml custard
Rub on head where hair is required.

b *Wart reducer lotion:*
350 ml pond water
50 ml beetroot juice
150 ml custard
200 ml ink
Spread on warts, leave for 7 days.

c *Verruca killer lotion:*
150 ml beetroot juice
250 ml custard
220 ml bath water
125 ml ink
Wash feet with lotion twice daily.

d *Nail strengthening lotion:*
550 ml pond water
250 ml beetroot juice
350 ml custard
425 ml bath water
375 ml ink
Dip hands into this for 1 hour.

2 **The professor makes each of his recipes. How much of each bottle of ingredients does he have left?**

3 **Use the rest of the ingredients to invent your own lotion or potion. What is it for? How much liquid do you make?**

Do not try this at home.

Using liquids

1 Work out the answer to each of these story sums.

a Jennifer has to take 10 ml of her medicine 4 times a day. She has a 250 ml bottle of medicine. How long will it last?

b 

A light aircraft burns 75 l of fuel every hour. How many litres of fuel are used on a 3-hour flight?

c A leaky tap drips 1.25 l of water every half hour. How much is wasted in 5 hours?

d 

A small car uses 1.75 l of petrol every 10 miles. How much does it use to travel 200 miles?

2 How can you use these buckets to measure 4 litres of water?

Cubic centimetres

Volume is the amount of space occupied by an object.

The volume of each cube is one cubic centimetre ($1\,cm^3$).

What is the volume of Sean's cuboid?

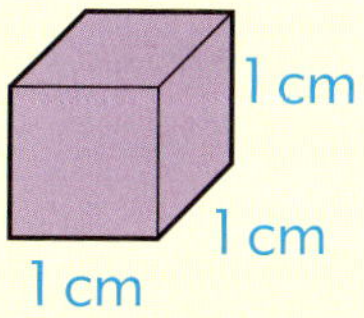

Sean has made the cuboid with cubes.

He has 6 cubes on the top layer.
He has 3 layers of 6 cubes.
$6 \times 3 = 18$
The volume of Sean's cuboid is $18\,cm^3$.

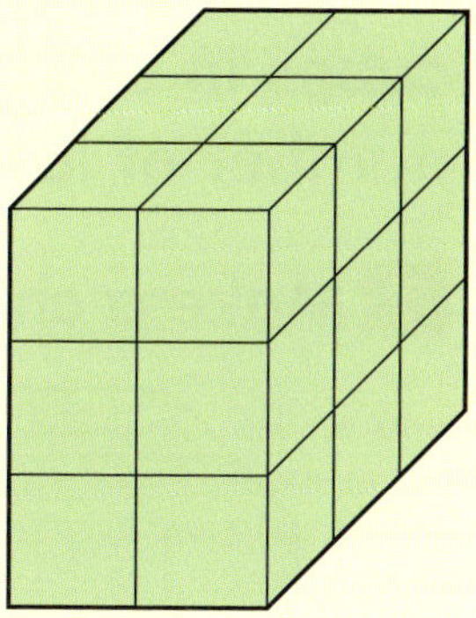

Build these shapes with centimetre cubes. Find the volume of each. Write it in cubic centimetres (cm^3).

1

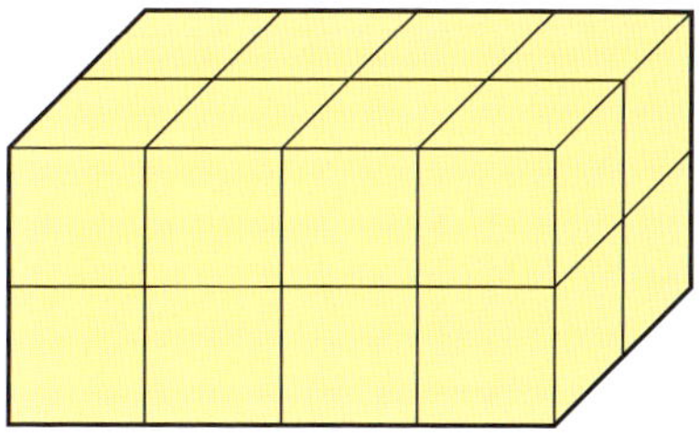

2

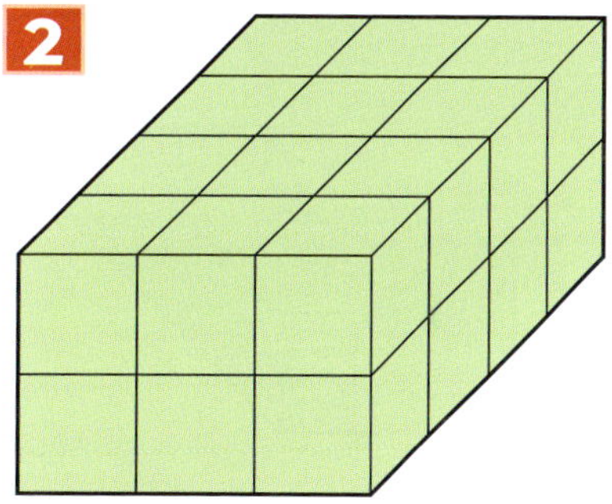

3

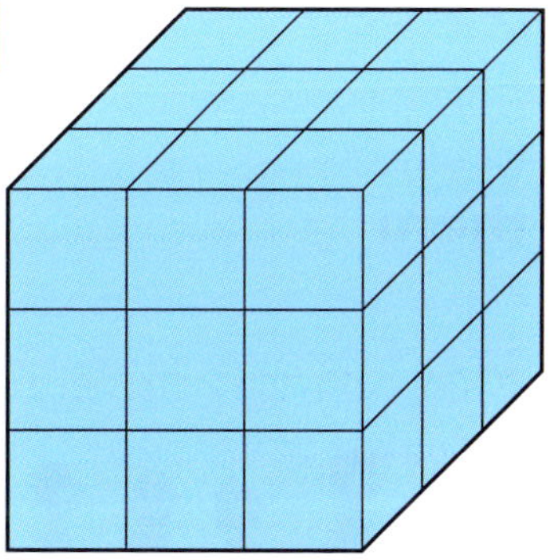

4

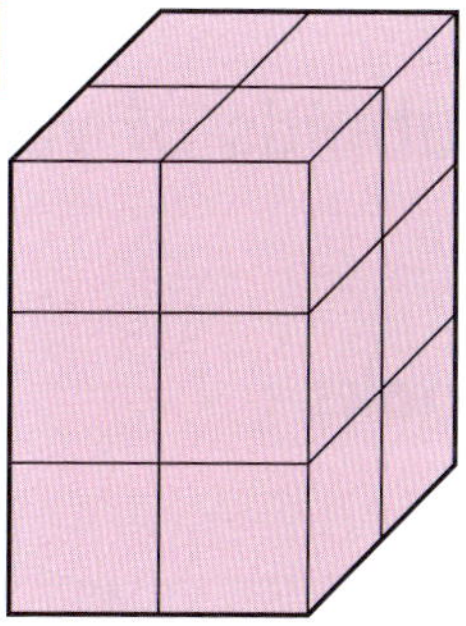

5

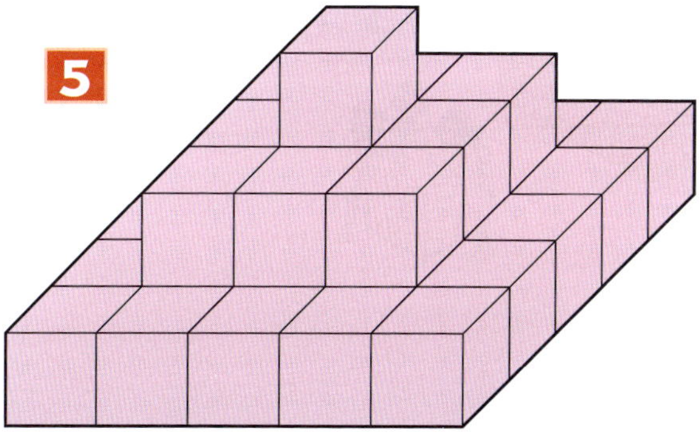

6

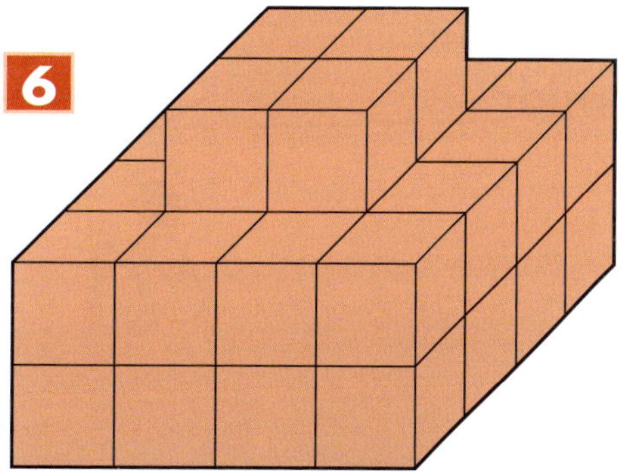

Recording volumes

This chart shows how the volume of a cuboid is related to the number of cubes in each layer and the number of layers.

Number of cubes in layers	Number of layers	Volume of cuboid
12	3	36 cm^2

1 Make a chart of these cuboids.

a

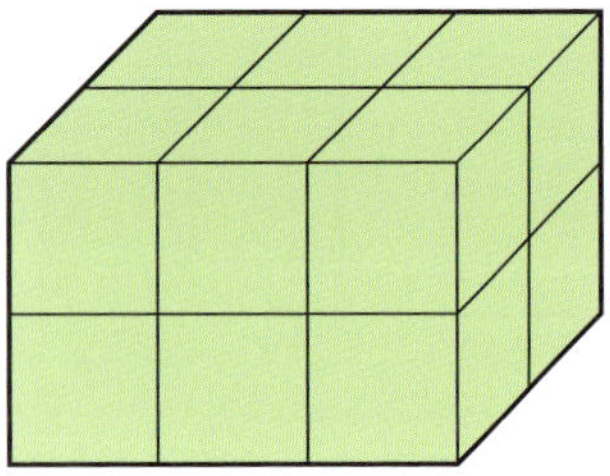

b

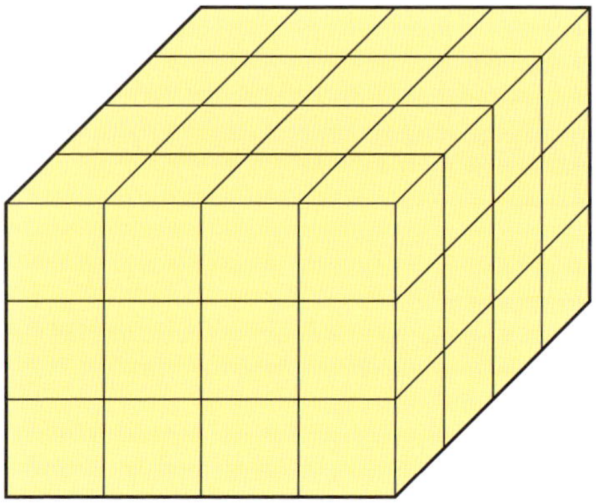

c

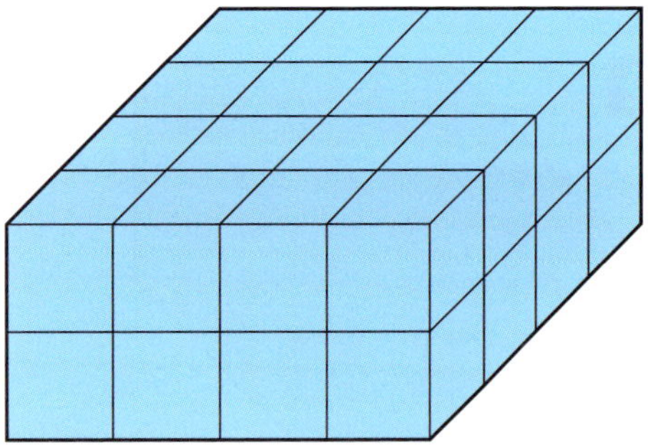

d

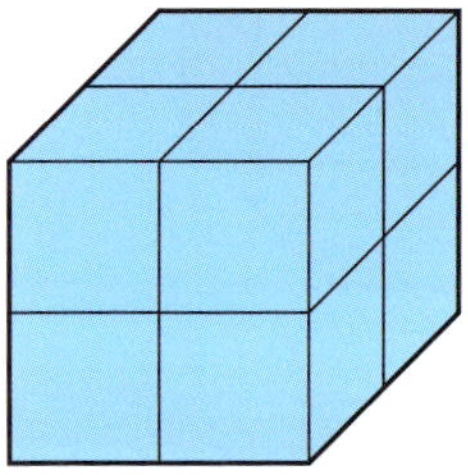

2 Make some cuboids of your own and add them to the chart.

3 How many blocks were needed to build the whole of the pyramid?

Length, breadth, height

Remember: Volume is the amount of space a shape occupies.

This cuboid has a length of 4 cm, a breadth of 3 cm and height of 2 cm.

Its volume is 24 cm^3.

$4\,cm \times 3\,cm \times 2\,cm = 24\,cm^3$

length × breadth × height = volume

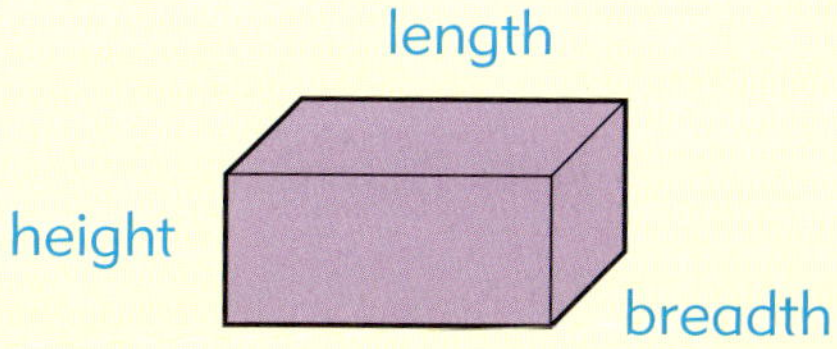

1 **Use length × breadth × height to find the volumes of these cuboids.**

a

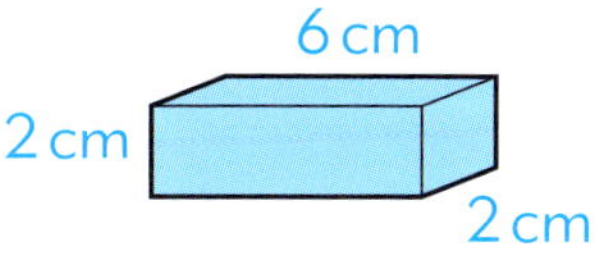

b

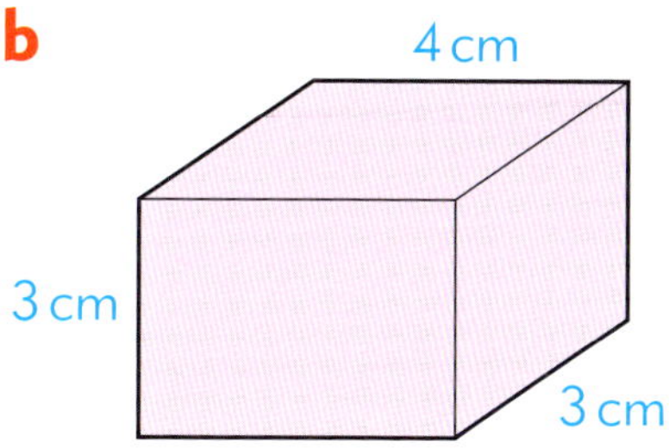

c

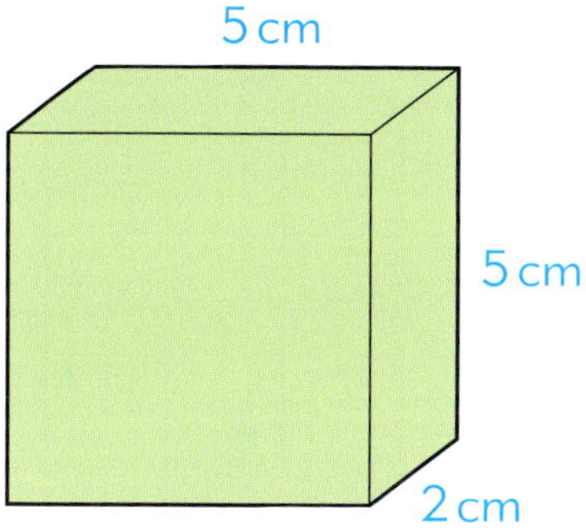

d

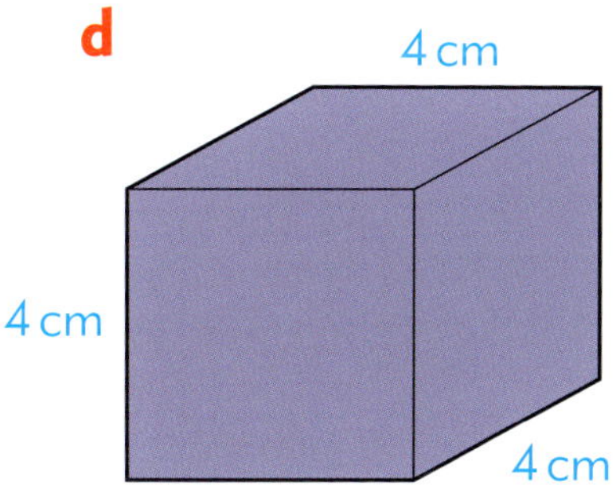

e

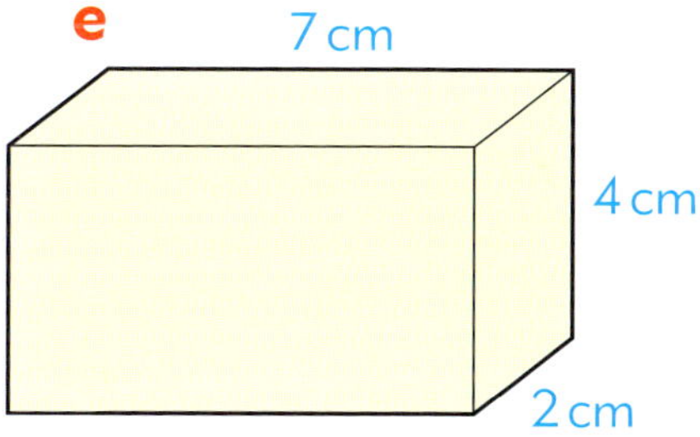

f

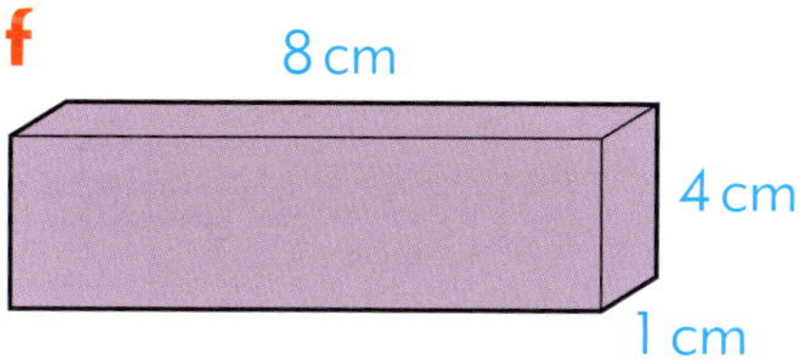

2 **On each of these cuboids, either the length, breadth or height is missing. Write down the missing measurement.**

a

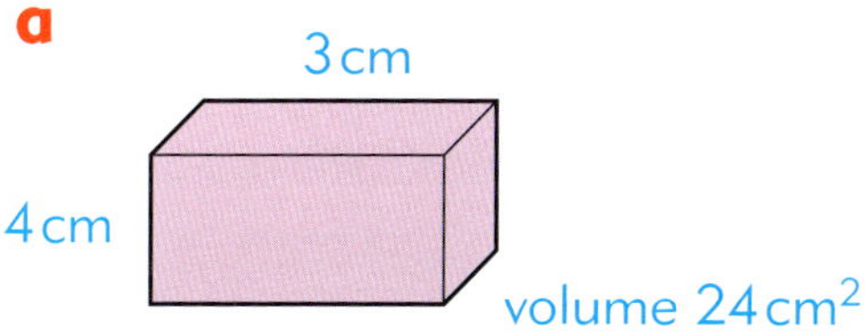

b

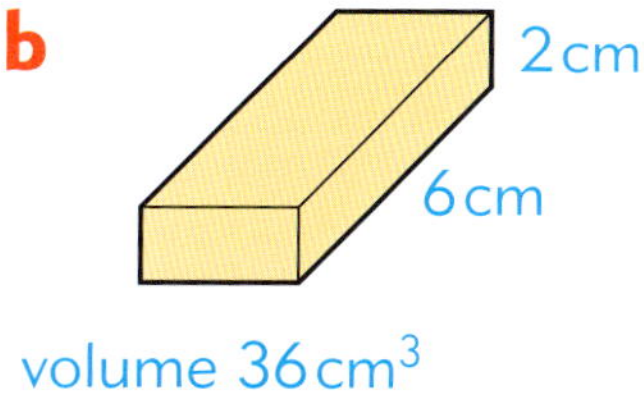

c

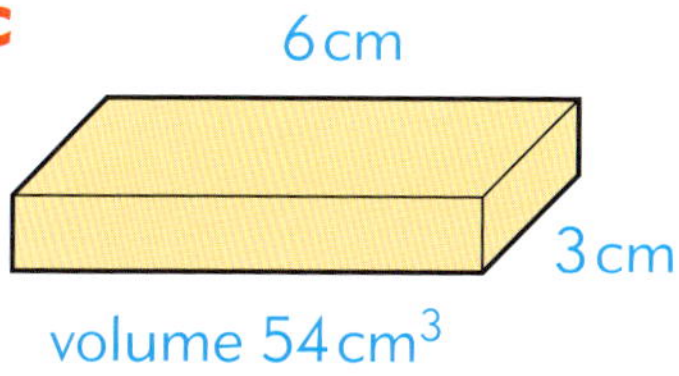

Finding pairs

These shapes each have a partner with the same volume. Work out the volume of each shapes. Write down the numbers for each pair.

1

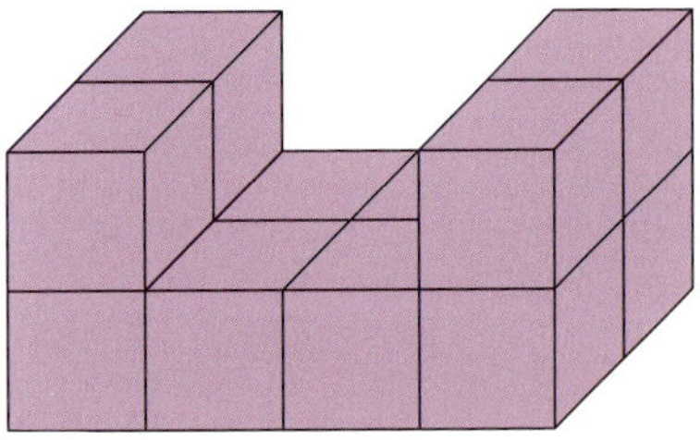

2

3

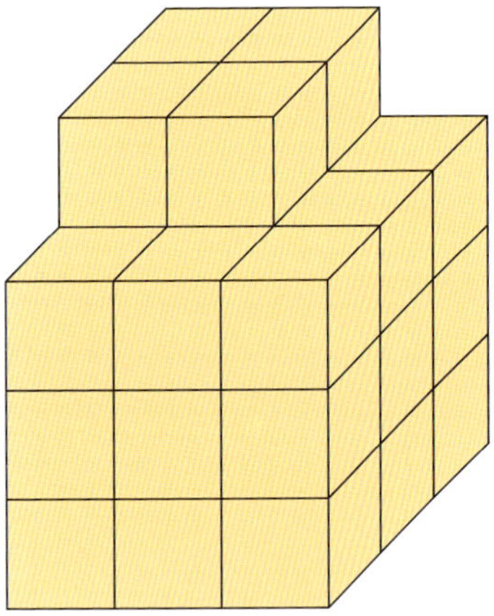

4

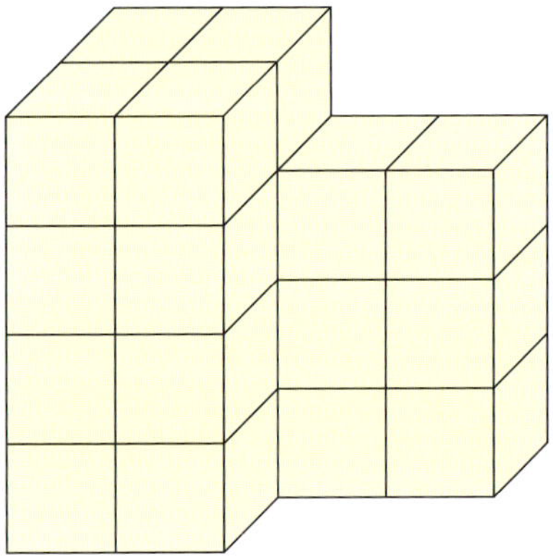

5

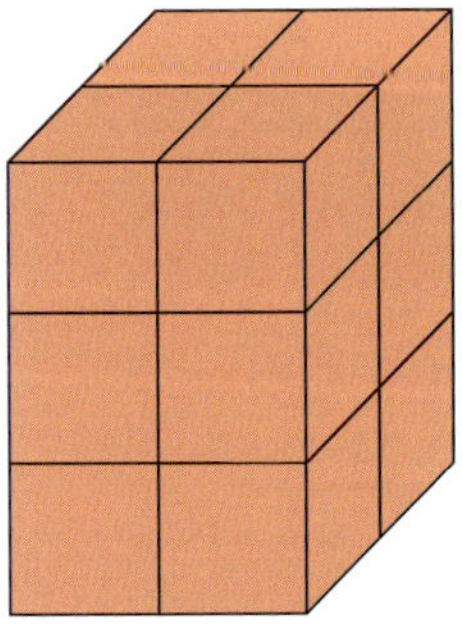

6

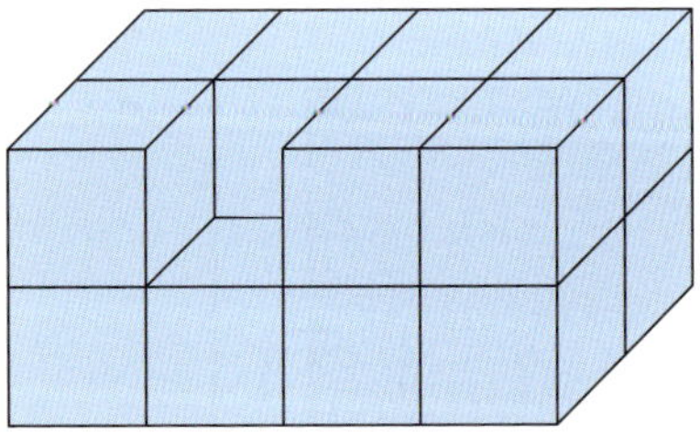

7

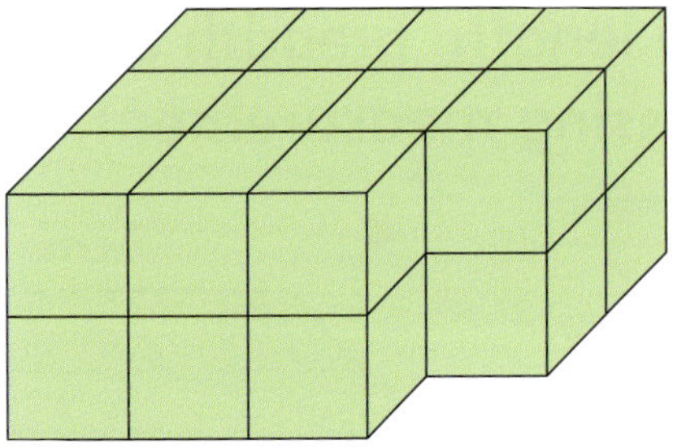

8

Capacity and volume

This is a net of a cuboid.

When the cuboid is made it has a length of 2 cm, a breadth of 2 cm and a height of 1 cm.

Its volume is

$2\,\text{cm} \times 2\,\text{cm} \times 1\,\text{cm} = 4\,\text{cm}^3$

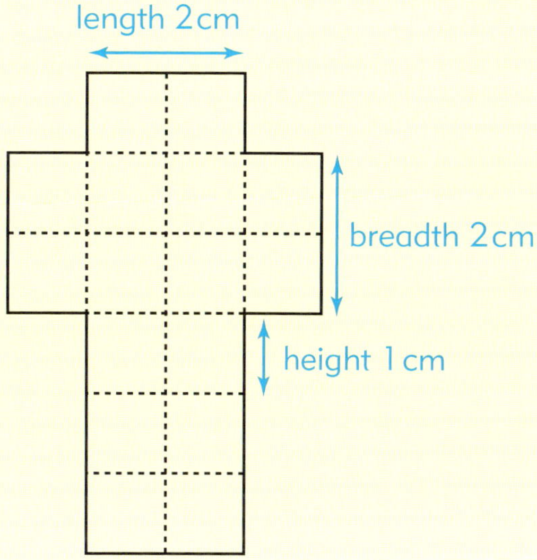

These nets can also be made into cubes and cuboids. Each square represents 1 square centimetre. Write their volumes.

1

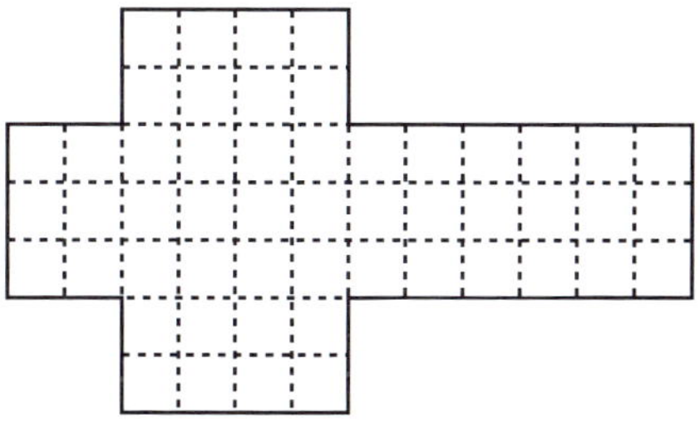

2

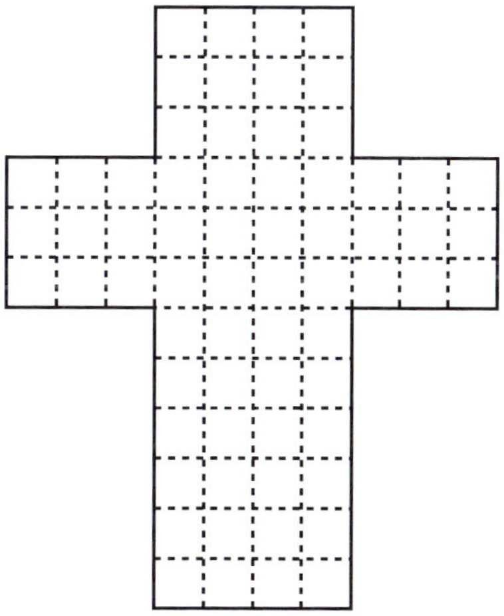

3

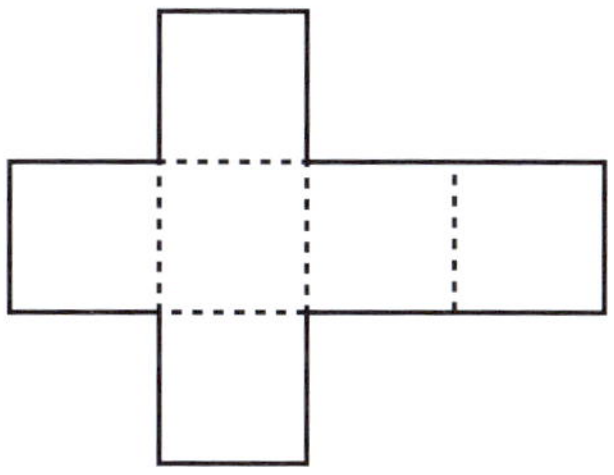

4

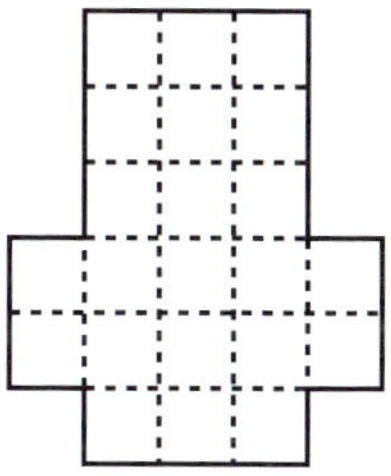

5

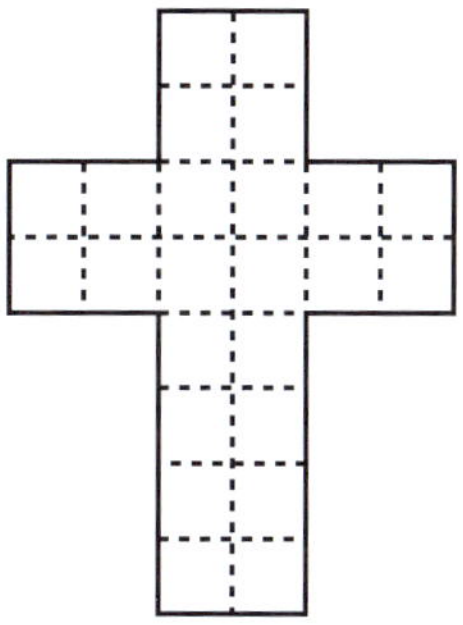

6

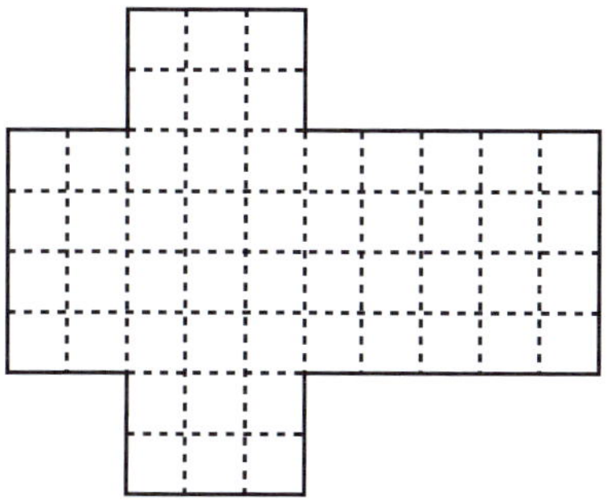

How much?

1 ml of water takes up 1 cm^3 of space and weighs 1 g.

This tank was filled with 500 ml of water.

A 3 cm × 3 cm × 3 cm cube was put into it.

Its volume of 27 cm^3 displaced 27 ml of water.

Displace means 'take the place of'.

27 ml of water overflowed.

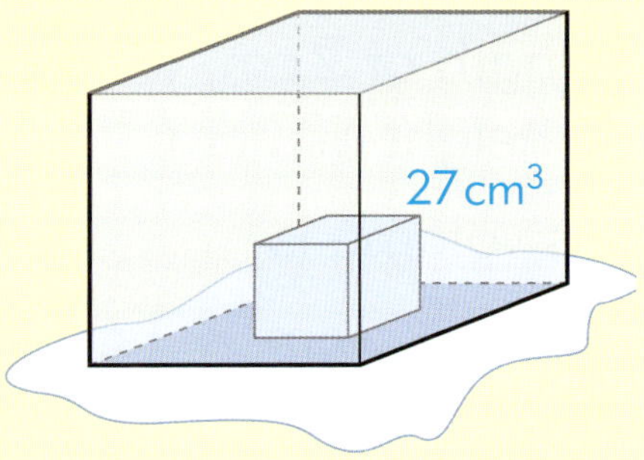

1 **How much water would these cubes and cuboids displace?**

a 10 cm × 6 cm × 2 cm

b 13 cm × 8 cm × 4 cm

c 11 cm × 16 cm × 2 cm

d 9 cm × 3 cm × 3 cm

e 12 cm × 5 cm × 4 cm

f 14 cm × 6 cm × 5 cm

2 **You can find the volumes of all sorts of everyday objects.**

Fill a displacement bucket with water. Place the object in it and use a measuring cylinder to measure the water that overflows.

Try these:

a a brick

b your hand

c a pair of scissors.

Remember to do this outside!

Elements of a set

Set A = {all flat shapes}

Which of the following are elements of Set A?

cuboid	rectangle	ball	circle
✗	✓	✗	✓

1 Set Q = {multiples of 5 from 0 to 50}

List all the elements of set Q.

2 Set S = {all shapes with four or fewer corners}

Say which of the following shapes do not belong to Set S.

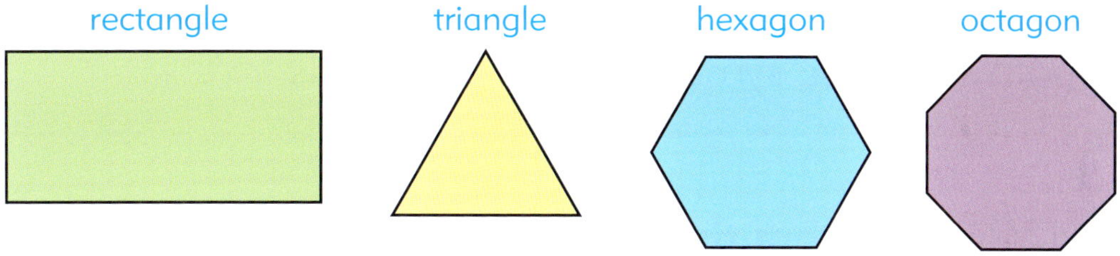

3 Play this game.

Everyone stands up. Your teacher will call out the properties of the standing set. Everyone else must sit down. Some examples of sets:

- everyone who is wearing glasses
- girls only
- boys only
- everyone who likes chocolate
- everyone who had cereal for breakfast.

Venn diagrams

Venn diagrams are a way of showing sets of items.

Set A = {the numbers 0 to 10}

Set B = {odd numbers up to 15}

The elements of set A are:
0, 1, 2, 3, 4, 5, 6, 7, 8, 9, 10

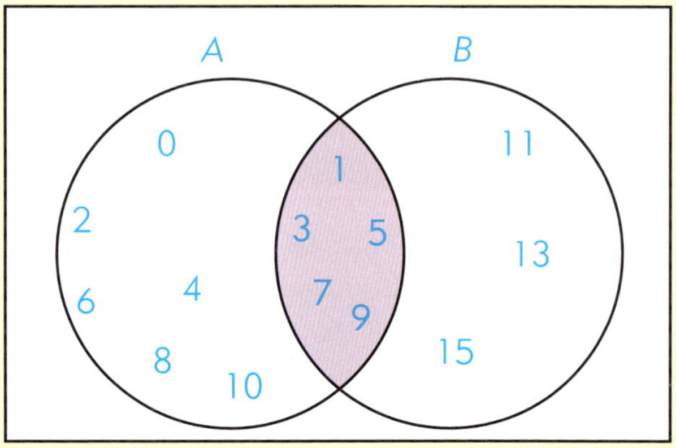

Another way of writing this is:

$A = \{0, 1, 2, 3, 4, 5, 6, 7, 8, 9, 10\}$

$A \cup B = \{0, 1, 2, 3, 4, 5, 6, 7, 8, 9, 10, 11, 13, 15\}$

The **union** of A and B means everything that is in either of the sets. '$\cup$' is the symbol for union.

$A \cap B = \{1, 3, 5, 7, 9\}$

The **intersection** of the sets means only the elements that belong to both sets. The symbol for intersection is '$\cap$'.

1 **Draw a Venn diagram that shows:**

Set A = {multiples of 2 up to 20}
Set B = {multiples of 3 up to 20}

2 **Set D = {names of the days of the week}**
Set E = {names of the days of the month}
Set F = {words beginning with S}

a List all the elements of set D.

b List all the elements of set E.

c Which elements from set D and set E would also appear in set F?

d Draw the intersection of sets E and F.
You don't have to fill in all the elements of set F.

you can use Workbook page 78

Carroll diagrams

Sofia made this chart about the children in her class. It is called a Carroll diagram.

	Boy	**Girl**
Has brown eyes	John Mahmoud David Kyle	Jenny Ella Maria Yasmina
Does not have brown eyes	Adam Ismael Ed Tony	Sofia Chloë

You will need:

- cardboard
- tape or string
- sticky tac
- pens
- small cards or soft strips of paper.

1 **Take a big piece of cardboard. Stick two pieces of coloured tape or string on your board to make a big Carroll diagram. Leave space at the top and on the left for labels. Make strips of paper with all the names of the people in your class.**

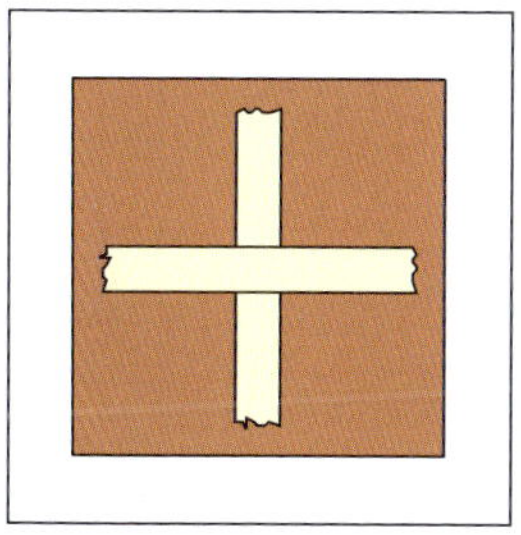

a Make four cards:

Boy	Girl	Has brown eyes	Does not have brown eyes

Stick the cards in the correct positions on the diagram.

Then arrange the name strips on the board.

b Think of different ways of sorting the children in your class. For example:

- Boys and girls who do and don't wear glasses.
- Boys and girls who do or don't like sport.

you can use Workbook page 79

Assessment 4

1 What percentage of each square is shaded?

a

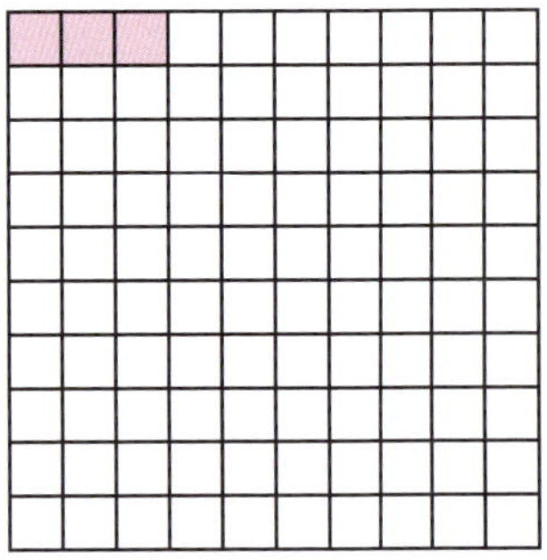

b

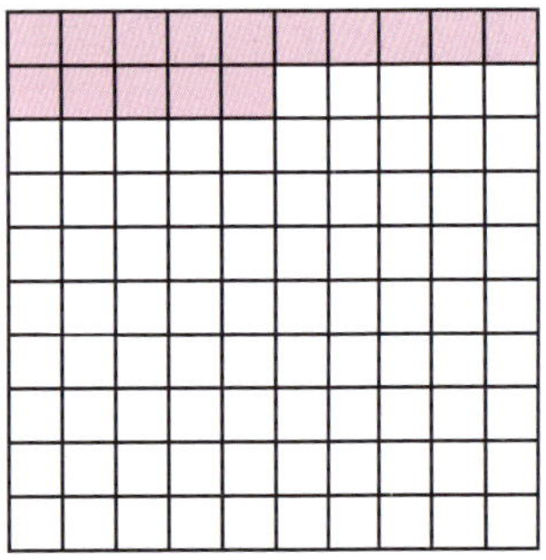

c

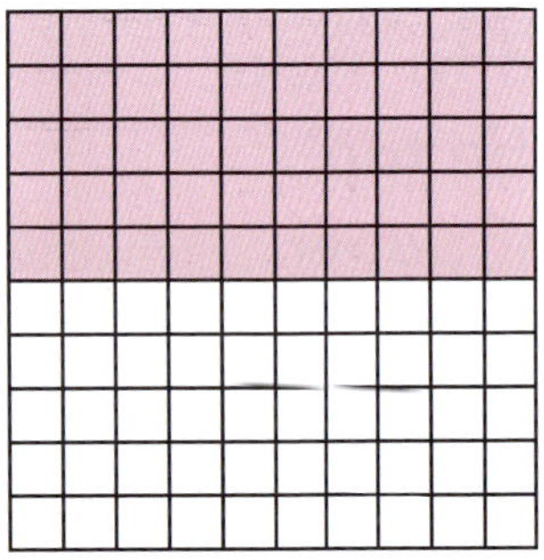

2 There are 24 pupils in our class. 12 are boys and the rest are girls. 6 pupils have green eyes. The rest have blue eyes. Write the percentage that:

a are boys

b are girls

c have green eyes

d have brown eyes

3 Find the area of each shape.

a □ = 1 cm^2

b

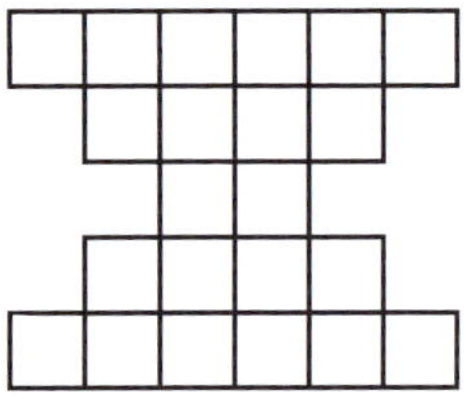

c

4 Write a sentence to define each kind of triangle below. Draw a sketch to illustrate an example of each.

a isosceles

b scalene

c equilateral

5 Can a right-angled triangle be scalene? Draw a triangle to check your answer.

Assessment 4

6 **For each angle, say whether it is less than, equal to or greater than a right angle.**

a

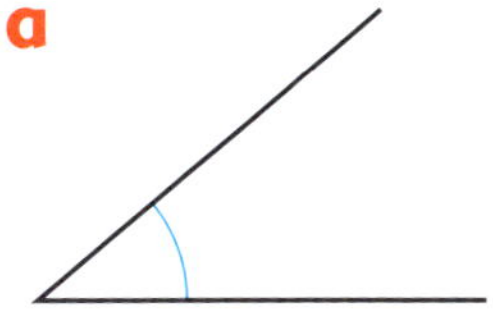

b

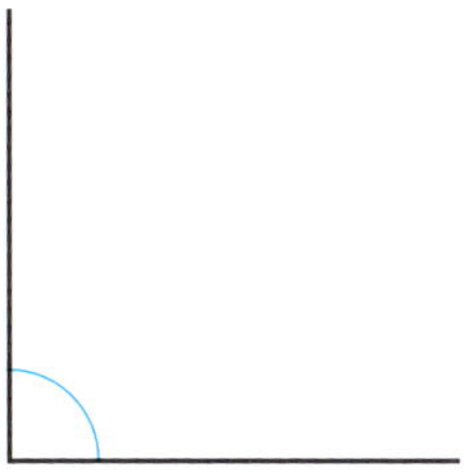

c

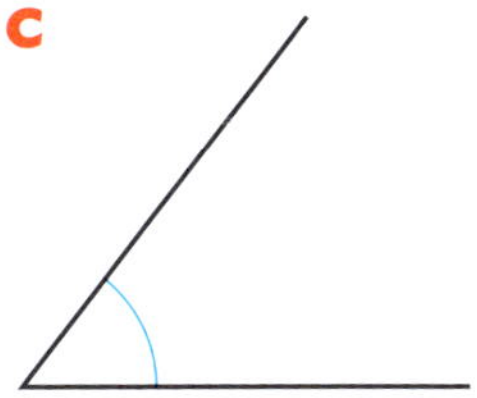

d

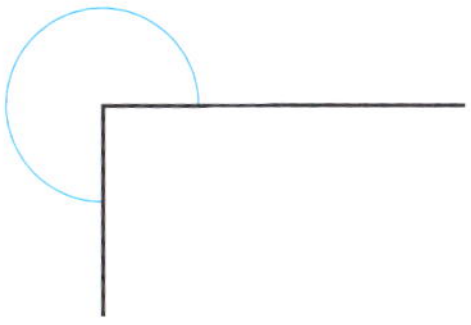

e

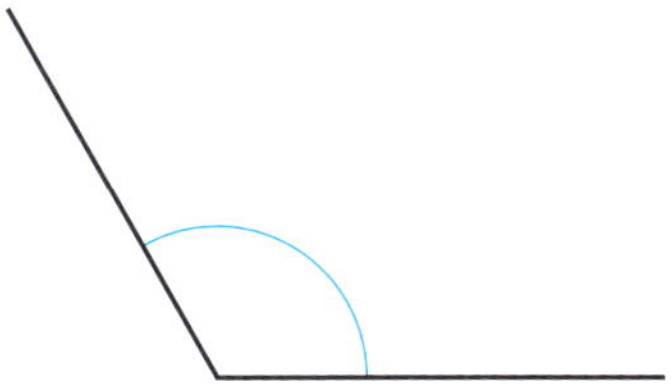

f

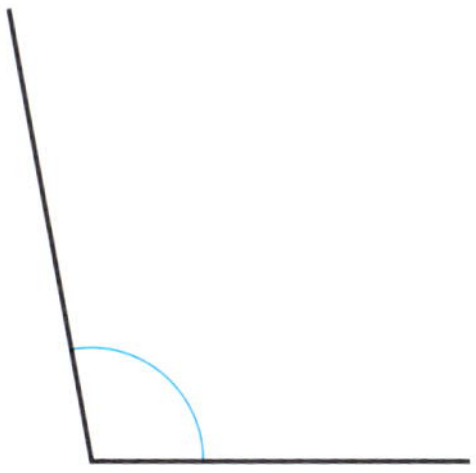

7 **$x = 10$ and $y = 15$. Solve these problems:**

a the sum of x and y

b the difference between x and y

c the product of x and y

d half of x multiplied by $\frac{1}{3}$ of y

e the difference between double x and double y.

8 **How many:**

a metres in a kilometre?

b cups in a litre?

c centimetres in a metre?

d grams in a kilogram?

e millilitres in a cup?

f millilitres in a litre?

9 **a** Write the elements of each set.

A = {whole numbers greater than 30 and less than 45}

B = {the first ten multiples of 5}

C = {the first ten multiples of 10}

b Write the elements of $A \cap B$.
(**Remember:** '$A \cap B$' means the intersection of sets A and B, or the elements they have in common.)

c Write the elements of $B \cap C$.

d Write the elements of $A \cap B \cap C$.

Assessment 4

10 W = {days of the week}

F = {words starting with F}

M = {months of the year}

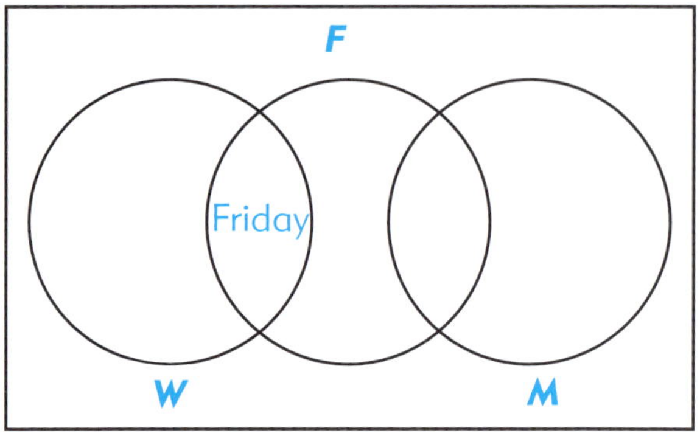

a Copy and complete the Venn diagram by filling in all the elements of sets **W** and **M** in the correct places.

b Fill in any five elements of set **F**.

c Is it possible to fill in all the elements of set **F**? Give a reason for your answer.

11 **Look at this Carroll diagram about the number of T-shirts sold at a shop over a weekend. Answer the questions that follow.**

Types of T-shirt sold at a shop

	Has words	Does not have words
White	𝍸 𝍸	|||
Not white	𝍸 𝍸 𝍸 |||	𝍸 𝍸 |||

a What are the four categories shown on this Carroll diagram?

b In which category would a green T-shirt with a picture of a dinosaur belong?

c Which was the most popular category?

d Which were more popular: T-shirts with words or T-shirts without words?

e Which were more popular: white T-shirts or T-shirts in other colours?

Glossary

A

Analogue clock – a clock that shows the time using hands which point to numbers arranged in a circle

Array – all the items in a set laid out so you can see them all – for example, an array of multiplication sums with the product 24

B

Bar graph – a graph where bars are used to show numbers or measurements

Block graph – a graph where columns are in blocks; each block shows one thing

C

Centimetre (cm) – a unit of length, your thumb is about 1 cm wide

Circle – a round, flat shape

Clockwise – the direction in which the hands move forwards in a circle around the face of an analogue clock; the opposite direction is called anti-clockwise

Cone – a solid shape with a pointed end and flat circular face

Co-ordinate – point on a grid

Cube – a solid shape with all its faces square

Cuboid – a solid shape with six faces; all the faces are rectangles

Cylinder – a solid shape with two circular end faces; a tin is a cylinder

D

Database – a chart containing information arranged in fields

Degree (°) – the unit used for measuring angles and temperature

Digital clock – a clock that shows the time using only numbers

Divide – share equally into groups

E

Estimate – a guess, what you think an answer will be

F

Fraction – a part; one half, one quarter and one third are all fractions

Frequency – how often something occurs

G

Geo-board – board with a grid of nails or pegs for making polygons

Gram (g) – a unit of mass used for light objects

H

Half – when you share things equally into two parts, each part is one half

Hexagon – a flat shape with six sides

Horizontal – a line that goes from one side to the other, parallel to the horizon

Hour – a measure of time: there are 60 minutes in one hour

K

Kilogram (kg) – a unit of mass used for heavy objects

Glossary

L

Litre (l) – a unit of capacity, how much a container holds

M

Metre (m) – a unit of length used for large measurements

Millimetre (mm) – a unit of length used for small measurements

Minute – a measure of time: there are 60 minutes in one hour

Mixed number – a number containing a whole number and a fraction

N

Negative numbers – numbers less than zero

Net – a flat shape that folds to enclose a 3-D solid

P

Pentagon – a flat shape with five sides

Pictogram – a type of graph where pictures are used to show information

Polygon – a flat shape with straight sides

Prism – a solid shape that is the same all the way through

Protractor – an instrument we use to measure angles

Pyramid – a solid shape with a flat base and faces that meet at a point

Q

Quadrilateral – a flat shape with four sides

Quarter – one of four equal parts of a whole; when you divide something into four equal parts each part is one quarter

R

Rectangle – a four-sided shape with four right-angled corners and opposite sides equal

Reflection – a mirror image or flip

Remainder – the number left over after division

Right angle – a quarter turn, like the corner of this page

Round off – to change a number to a lower place value to make it easier to work with. For example, we can round a number to the nearest ten, 100 or 1000

S

Second – a unit of time: there are 60 seconds in one minute

Sphere – a solid round shape; a ball is a sphere

Square – a four-sided flat shape with all sides equal

Subtract – take away or minus

Symbol – a picture used to represent something on a pictogram

Symmetrical – able to be divided into two identical parts

T

Tally – a small mark used to count one object; every fifth mark is drawn across the previous four tallies 卌

Third – a fraction, one of three equal parts; if you divide something into three equal parts, each part is one third

Triangle – a flat shape with three sides

V

Vertical – a line that goes straight up and down, perpendicular to the horizon